SEDUCED

THE GROOMING OF AMERICA'S TEENAGERS

OPAL S. SINGLETON

www.xulonpress.com

DEDICATION

This book is dedicated to

Del Singleton: my husband, my partner, my best friend. This incredibly intelligent, patient, and supportive man has joined me in my journey of long hours of research and listened to hundreds of presentations as we have committed our lives to helping families keep their kids safe from exploitation.

It is also dedicated to the hundreds of men and women across America who go undercover to go against the worst of the worst – men and women who exploit other people's bodies for financial gain and personal power.

Finally – this is dedicated to the "Best of the Best".

The men and women of RCAHT
(Riverside County Anti-Human Trafficking Task Force)
Aron, Sarge, Danny, Brian, Nancy, Christine.

ENDORSEMENTS

For many years Opal Singleton has been tracking trends in human trafficking and the sexual exploitation of some of our planet's most vulnerable people. She has built on her first-hand observations of Southeast Asia's sex trade and has expanded on that considerable body of knowledge with her work alongside law enforcement in Southern California's Inland Empire. Most recently, she has been helping victims of criminal street gangs to recover their dignity, reunite with their families and re-start their lives. Now, Opal has published a terrifying account, describing just how vulnerable American children and teens are to sexual predators that target and groom them for prostitution and exploitation. This book is a must-read for parents and for anyone interested in knowing more about the dangers of our new, wired world.

—Chief Sergio Diaz, Riverside Police Department

Opal is truly a general in this war to protect our youth from exploitation. Sex trafficking has devastated the lives of children and families around the world and we are just now touching the surface of this insidious crime. Opal has provided cutting edge information to thousands about pervasiveness of human trafficking, and through this book, many more. I've had the advantage of working with Opal on the "john" side of trafficking, and cannot recommend a more qualified expert in this area. For parents, law enforcement, or anyone serving the needs of our youth, this book is a MUST READ! —-David Stewart, LMFT

Of all the people that I know who are combating human trafficking, no one knows more about this issue than Opal Singleton. She is an indefatigable champion of protecting children and restoring survivors. —Kerry Decker, Pastor, Author, and Human Rights Activist

I have had the privilege of serving alongside Opal Singleton in the fight against child slavery and sexual exploitation for many years as Opal serves on the board of Rapha House. Opal is a tireless crusader in the prevention of child trafficking and the education of communities against exploitation. Her desire for excellence in her work has led her into deep research to uncover new breeding grounds for predators to recruit victims. *Seduced* is an eye opening and thought-provoking book which will inspire us all to become educated and to take action. This is a must read for all of us who have children who are special to us and for those with a passion to end child exploitation. —-Stephanie Freed, Executive Director, Rapha House International

Opal works with young people as if they were her very own. Her expertise and sincerity is what shines through. She puts forth her heart and soul into saving tomorrow's mothers. She is at the top of my list as a Super Hero. Speaking as someone she has influenced with her vast knowledge and training skills, she has made me a more effective advocate. Jeanetta McAlpin, CEO, Overground Railroad. Former Women's and Children's Commissioner, Long Beach, California.

TABLE OF CONTENTS

FOREWORD

By Andrew Doan, MD, PhD

In the digital age, humans are connected through online gaming, Internet chat rooms, and mobile devices. For the most part, technology facilitates incredible advances in communication, medicine, science, business, and many facets of our modern world. Through working with Opal Singleton, I have become aware of how predators can utilize technology to groom and steal our children away for sex trafficking.

As a scientist who focuses on research studying why people use technology excessively, I am aware of the biological pathways that provide feedback, reward, and reinforcement of behaviors associated with technology use. As a clinician who studies addictive behaviors, I have witnessed firsthand people who use technology excessively to the point of dysfunction. As a parent, I have observed how technology infiltrates and consumes my own children if healthy boundaries are ignored. Undeniably, technology influences and reprograms human behaviors and neuronal pathways. These behaviors can either be bad or good, depending on the rewiring.

The problem is when the majority of children are using technology excessively, without healthy boundaries. It is estimated that the average child eight to eighteen years of age is using a digital screen for entertainment purposes an average of seven hours and thirty-eight minutes daily (Kaiser Family Foundation, 2010). On the other hand, the benefits of moderate use of video games have been well documented, such as improving hand-eye coordination, facilitating pro-social behaviors, and enhancing emotional stability (Przybylski, 2014). For example, children who play one hour or less of video games daily exhibit higher satisfaction with life, pro-social behavior, and lower externalizing and internalizing of problems than children who do not play video games. The opposite was found for children playing three hours or more daily (Przybylski, 2014). Dr. Donald Hebb, a Canadian neuroscientist, described the basic mechanism for synaptic plasticity in 1949 (Hebb, 1949): a simple phrase that characterizes this mechanism is "neurons that fire together, wire together" (Doidge, 2007). A corollary to this mechanism is "use it or lose it." The brain is organized into numerous cortical columns. These columns change via neuronal plasticity, mediated by immediate early genes (IEGs), such as *c-myc*, *c-fos*, and *c-jun*. These IEGs are transcription factors mediating expression of proteins involved in synaptogenesis and neuronal connections. Repeated behaviors strengthen the neuronal pathways associated with the behaviors, while neuronal pathways associated with less utilized behaviors are not strengthened.

Human beings practice who they want to become, and individuals must be careful what they practice and how they program their brains. When a young child spends too much time in Internet gaming or Internet activities, there can be significant problems. We propose an analogy to clarify how a child's nervous system may develop when exposed to excessive time engaging in Internet gaming or other Internet activities. Observe your left hand. The thumb will represent the cortical areas associated with all the benefits of video gaming and use of technology: quick analytical skills, improved hand-eye-coordination, and perhaps improved reflexes. The index finger will represent the cortical areas associated with communication skills. The middle finger will represent behaviors associated with social bonding with family and friends. The ring finger will represent the capacity to recognize emotions of both self and others (empathy). Lastly, the little finger will represent the cortical areas associated with self-control. While these higher executive functions are biologically based, they are not fully expressed without proper practice and feedback. When a child spends on average of seven hours and thirty-eight minutes in front of a digital screen for entertainment, that child is exceeding the recommended daily dosage for healthy screen time (Przybylski, 2014). Folding the fingers into the palm of your hand represents this situation. As the brain matures, the possible end product is a young adult who is *all thumbs* in their thinking: possessing quick analytical skills and quick reflexes, but not as developed in communication skills, having few bonds with people, exhibiting little empathy, and showing minimal self-control.

It is my opinion and concern that children with this type of "all thumbs thinking" are the lowest hanging fruit to be online victims for human trafficking. Opal Singleton's book is ground breaking. Her book provides sobering and horrifying truths about how online predators use video games, online chat rooms, social medial, and cell phones to attract, lure, and groom our children to be online victims for a hundred billion dollar sex industry.

Andrew Doan MD PhD

www.andrew-doan.com

*Opinions and points of view expressed are those of the author's and do not necessarily reflect the official position or policies of the U.S. NAVY or the Department of Defense.

References

Doidge, N. (2007). The Brain That Changes Itself. *United States: Viking Press*, 427.

Hebb, D. (1949). The Organization of Behavior. *New York: Wiley and Sons.*

KaiserFamilyFoundation. (2010). Generation M2: Media in the Lives of 8- to 18-Year-Olds. http://kff.org/other/event/generation-m2-media-in-the-lives-of/.

Przybylski, A. K. (2014). Electronic Gaming and Psychosocial Adjustment. *Pediatrics.*

OPAL SINGLETON: MY JOURNEY

I wrote this book because I care. I work in combating child sex trafficking in the U.S. and Southeast Asia. Most people think human trafficking is primarily about kidnapping or dealing with coyotes trying to bring foreigners into our country. It is not. Seventy-two percent of human trafficking cases in California are U.S. citizens. Most are our children being accessed, groomed, and recruited into "The Life."

Gangs, pimps, and predators seek out the vulnerable: foster children, homeless children, runaway children, pregnant teens and *all kids* on the Internet who make themselves available. I sit with parents who are looking for their missing children. I talk with guys and girls who are being blackmailed and recruited because they sent a naked photo to their newfound friend. I make presentations to government officials, corporations, civic groups, churches, and the public nearly seventy hours a week. I drive 3,000-4,000 miles a month.

Most people say, "How did you get into this?" I cannot tell you for sure, but I do know God guides me, every day, one foot in front of the other.

I am retired. My background is international marketing. I retired in 2000 after losing my right balance nerve (Meniere's Disease). I had accrued nearly three million frequent flyer miles. For many years, I became an artist and relaxed. Then one day I started to attend a church with a mission in Cambodia and I began to get involved.

I am an avid researcher. I spent weeks researching everything I could on sex trafficking in Asia and the U.S. There was little information available on sex trafficking in the U.S.

In 2010, we began to see human trafficking in Riverside County, California. God placed me in a position to meet an undercover deputy who had just formed a task force. His job was to find a human trafficker in a 7,200-square-mile county. His name was Aron Wolfe. We quickly determined that I might be helpful. He asked me to volunteer, pay all my own way, raise my own funds, and train the public about human trafficking so that we could find leads.

I sat at my kitchen table and began by asking, "What does human trafficking look like in the U.S.?" I started in Coachella Valley, where Mexican migrants are brought in as seasonal workers for agriculture. I gathered facts and met with farmers and the Department of Agriculture, and started attending Farm Bureau dinners. (My husband started to think I might have a boyfriend, because that is weird if you are not a farmer.) I learned about migrant trafficking and created a training program with my pastor, Kerry Decker. Fortunately for me, he is an outstanding graphic artist, because at that stage I could barely make my own PowerPoint presentations. I trained our county code enforcement officers to monitor for vacant houses because they are often used for temporary brothels. I trained animal control agents because gangs and cartels often use dogs for security on drop houses. I trained alcoholic beverage control officers because often foreign national girls are used as "B" girls (bar girls) who are forced to give lap dances to bar clients in strip clubs without pay.

To this day, I read every child sex trafficking case in the U.S. and every child porn exploitation case in the world through Google Alerts. I want to teach myself how all of this happens, because almost every time it is different. Predators change their tactics. Pimps are opportunists and they will take the low road every time, but the low road changes. I had the advantage of working with the Riverside Sheriff Department and seeing cases. As I became a well-known public speaker, people told me their personal experiences. Some needed sharing. We must learn from each other so this does not have to happen to another young person.

Then in late 2011 or early 2012, we had a significant case of child sex trafficking that changed my life. A beautiful young girl with a two-parent household was recruited into prostitution in her high school by another girl. This recruiter is called a "bottom girl". A local gang placed a gang girl into one of the best high schools in Riverside for the sole purpose of recruiting children into prostitution. The night this case broke open and it appeared in the paper, I was giving a presentation to the public about human trafficking. To this day, I always train to the latest case, and that night I showed a video from television about this case. When it was over, two beautiful ladies came forward and told me that the girl in the video was their daughter/granddaughter. They began to tell me how it all looked to them as a family. They told me how their beautiful daughter changed before their eyes and they simply did not know what to do. These are incredibly beautiful,

God-loving people, all of them. Daughter, mother, and grandmother. Their daughter was recruited and forced into prostitution into the Rolling 60s Street Gang in Los Angeles for over nine months. This family fought hard to get their daughter back. Some families don't, sadly. Today, the girl is back and rebuilding her life. The girl is incredibly strong. She is my hero. They are an amazing family. I believe with all my heart that God gave me this experience so it could be used to change others' lives.

Shortly thereafter, I was called to Cambodia for a business matter. By that time I was serving on the Board of Rapha House International. This is the most amazing organization that rescues and restores trafficked children in Cambodia, Thailand, Myanmar, and Haiti. Stephanie Freed is the Executive Director. She has become a true confidant and friend. She may be the most dedicated person I have ever met, when it comes to rescuing girls from sex slavery.

At this time, God began to lay on my heart a training curriculum which I call, "The Love Trap." It is all about sex trafficking, how it works and how to prevent it. As I stood in Phnom Penh, looking out at a sea of over six hundred faces of beautiful Cambodian children, I began to realize that we create human trafficking prevention training programs for third world countries, why don't we do this for our children and parents in the U.S.? I served four months as the Acting Country Director of one of the largest safe houses in Cambodia, and what an amazing education and experience it was. I learned so much about the psychology of abuse and recruitment. The tactics of predators may be different in Cambodia, but the trauma experienced by a trafficked twelve-year-old is the same. Maybe there are some cultural differences, but certainly the pain of exploitation is a lifelong scar. Many victims never recover.

When I returned to the U.S., I returned to volunteering with the sheriff's department. I began delivering The Love Trap training program to every church, government agency, rotary, AAUW, Soroptomist, and other groups that would invite me. I talked to anyone who would listen. Some were kind enough to take up an offering or make a donation to help cover the cost of gas. I am grateful for those who have supported me financially. Today, The Love Trap has been delivered to Over 50,000 people. In 2012, the Riverside Police Chief, Sergio Diaz, asked if I would train school officials in his city. He is a true visionary. I was reluctant. I feared parents protesting over my presentations on prostitution and pimping to their sweet little inno-cent darlings.

I was wrong. He opened the doors, and today we have led the nation in training about sex traf-ficking in the educational system within Riverside County. The Riverside Office of Education, the Riverside County Superintendent of Schools, and the leaders of California Safe Schools have been amazing. We train all school officials first, including principals, teachers and support staff such as coun-selors, school resource officers, nurses, psycholo-gists and most important, child welfare attendance officers (truancy officers), because one of the first indications that a child is being groomed and recruited is that they begin to miss school. Finally, we find a way to train the students and parents. Sometimes it is in classrooms, sometimes public assemblies, and sometimes in specialized school events. In every presentation, I have found that if you tell teenagers like it is, *they listen*.

In many training programs, we end up with leads to potential cases. Recently during a conference for high school teens, three girls came forward and showed us their smart phones, where they were being recruited. It is worth the effort.

By 2012, RCAHT (Riverside County Anti Human Trafficking Task Force) had developed into a full-fledged task force. They had begun to receive grants from Cal-OES and later the Department of Justice. Today, they are a task force of amazing men and women. The best of the best. These folks put their lives on the line to go after the worst of the worst. People who sell other people's bodies are the worst of the worst. I am so proud to represent this task force. I have learned so much from them. My boss, Sgt. John Sawyer, has been a true friend and confidant. He encourages me on those days when I get up and wonder if I can do this one more day. We make a great team. He leads incredible law enforcement officers, and my goal is to: 1.) Prevent sex trafficking and 2.) Educate others so we can obtain quality leads on potential traffickers for the RCAHT team. I spend hour upon hour making sure parents understand how to protect their children, and helping teens who are close to sliding off the edge of society to understand just how dark the wrong decision can get. In my experience, most teens have no understanding of how quickly their life can go from bored and mundane to painful devastation. In today's digital world, one bad decision can change your life.

In 2013, RCAHT received a Department of Justice grant that allocated funds for the Million Kids, non-profit organization, where I serve as president.

It is only part-time, but it allows me to raise the funds I need to cover the expenses to keep Million Kids functioning. I do this seventy hours a week, and if there is time or energy left I go on the Internet and look for children who are missing. Once you have sat with heartbroken parents looking for their missing child, you have no other alternative but to do everything you can with the knowledge you have to try to bring one more vulnerable child home.

I want to thank Operation Safehouse for being a great partner. They are the best victim service provider in the U.S assisting victims who have been exploited by sexual predators and traffickers. They are some of the early pioneers in rescue, restoration and healing of child sex trafficking survivors and I am fortunate to have been able to work with them over the past several years.

I want to acknowledge my personal counselor, Claudia Bouslough, Riverside LMFT. You cannot work in human exploitation without having a strong psychological counselor. Claudia is the best and gives me ways to deal with the despair that comes in recognizing that there are cases that just cannot be fixed. She keeps my glass half-full.

I also want to recognize Susie Carpenter, Media and Marketing Director of Million Kids. Without her, I would not be here today. She owns Figgyworks, an Internet marketing company. Susie researches and posts new articles several times a day on the Million Kids (Riverside) Facebook page. It is the most current information available to train yourself about human trafficking. Susie takes on other clients; so if you need the *best* Internet marketer, give her a call. Leave time for my business too, okay?

I want to acknowledge the time spent with Dr. Andrew Doan, Ph.D., MD and neuroscience researcher on addiction, and his wife, Julie. He wrote a book called *Hooked on Games,* which I highly recommend. Dr. Doan operates Real Battle Ministries, and we have developed a presentation together called "The End Game", which we present to universities, corporations, conferences, and mega churches. Much of my insights on the impact of online gaming and MMORPGs have come from long discussions with Andy and Julie. I am deeply indebted to them.

I also want to acknowledge David Stewart, LMFT in Riverside. David is a pornography and sex addiction counselor family therapist, and he has guided me in understanding how sex and pornography addiction can completely ensnare adults and teens alike. He helped me to understand how important it is that individuals struggling with addictions get professional counseling.

After many hours working with churches, God laid it on my heart to create a program called "Grace, Hope and Fatherhood". I am grateful to Tyndale Publishing for giving Million Kids a grant to create the program. This is a six-session training program on human trafficking, complete with scripture, a study guide, discussion questions, and six professional videos. It is downloaded at www.churchactionnetwork.com, and can be used for individual training or shared with Sunday school groups, women's groups, and larger scale audiences. The formal program was developed by Pastor Kerry Decker, international human trafficking activist, author, graphic artist, and pastor of Compass Christian Church in Riverside, California. I highly recommend this program to understand how the faith-based community can implement actionable programs that will prevent child sex trafficking. I also want to acknowledge Rees Evans for providing the professional voice-over services so that the videos are inspiring and concise and communicate the message of the need for grace and strong male role models in our quest to protect our children.

Kerry Decker is my pastor and was the visionary who started Million Kids. As Kerry began to focus on starting a new church in Riverside, he handed Million Kids to me. Kerry is still very much involved in helping foster children and helping at-risk and exploited youth around the globe. Compass Christian Church (Riverside), Flipside Church (Rancho Cucamonga), Hillside Church (Rancho Cucamonga), and Calvary Chapel Church (Rancho Cucamonga) have been loyal financial supporters of Million Kids and I am grateful. I am so busy with the work I struggle raising financing. They are the true heroes to put air under others' wings.

I want to acknowledge the most important contributor of all to this fight for our children's lives, Del Singleton, my husband. He is more than a husband and partner and friend. He is the most intelligent, insightful individual I have ever known. We spend long hours talking about each of the issues in this book. He often has insights that are critical. He has conducted research and helped with the administration of Million Kids. Time and again, he has sat through The Love Trap and Grace, Hope, and Fatherhood presentations. He understands when I need to be with a parent or take calls from a scared young person in the middle of dinner. When I needed to go to Cambodia, he came. He is as concerned about the grooming of America's teenagers as I am. I am truly blessed. Every day when I rise at four am (remember, we are both retired), he rolls over and lets me know I can follow God's

lead one more day. He has incredible humor and it is so empowering. He has given me the greatest gift one human being can give another.
He believes in me.

I wrote this book to get you thinking. I hope parents and grandparents will read it and realize that you can be as empowered as you choose to be. It is our children who are at stake. The journey starts by understanding what you don't know, and vowing that your children can teach you. Or you will teach yourself. It is a dialogue. You are never too old to learn. Only the naïve choose to be uninformed. In this day and age, you simply cannot choose to be naïve. Your children *need* you to be engaged with them.

Finally, Million Kids is a small public benefit, 501(c)3 non-profit organization. We pay all our own way. There is a desperate need to create electronic messaging and take this message across America. We need to create online training programs and blogs and YouTube videos so this training can be dispersed every day. Predators, pimps, and perpetrators change their MO daily; we must too. If after reading this book you want to help, you can. Tell five more people about this book and let's get America's parents and grandparents educated about the power of parenting in the Internet age. If you want a presentation to your corporation, large-scale church or college or university, please contact us. Follow us on Facebook and enroll in our blog to keep yourself informed. And share the message.

If you want to make a financial donation to us, we would greatly appreciate it. You can mail your donation or go to our web page:

Million Kids Riverside
PO Box 7295
Riverside, California 92513
WWW.MILLIONKIDS.ORG

FOLLOW US ON FACEBOOK:
MILLION KIDS RIVERSIDE
OPAL SINGLETON: *OSINGLE405@AOL.COM*

THANK YOU FROM THE BOTTOM OF MY HEART.
Your love and support mean the world to me.
I cannot do this alone.
Please share this message
with everyone you know.
Love, Opal

INTRODUCTION

**SEDUCED:**
TAKE ONE TWELVE-YEAR-OLD
ADD BIOLOGICAL CHANGES,
HORMONES RAGING
FRONTAL LOBE PARTIALLY DEVELOPED
DESPERATE NEED FOR PEER APPROVAL
HAND THEM A DEVICE WITH 24/7 ACCESS TO
THE ENTIRE WORLD
ADD VIOLENCE AND SEXUAL ANIMATION
LET THEM CREATE AN AVATAR (A FANTASY
CHARACTER IN A REAL WORLD)
OPEN THE DOOR TO NEARLY A MILLION
PREDATORS AROUND THE GLOBE TO
SUCCEED; HE NEEDS THE APPROVAL OF A
GUILD MANAGER
AND OTHER GUILD PLAYERS…WHO ARE
ALSO AVATARS

HOW ON EARTH COULD THAT GO WRONG?

Never before in history has there been so much competition to influence your child's morals, spirituality, sexuality, gender identity, self-image, and decision-making. We are at a unique time in the universe where perfectly normal parents hand their child a device that provides literally hundreds of thousands of unknown individuals around the globe access to their child's ideological formation 24/7. Until recently the parent was the single biggest influence in a young person's life. Proverbs 22:6 says, "Train up a child in the way he should go and when he is old, he will not depart from it." How does that work with all the latest technological advancements? Many parents only have access to their child about fifteen percent of the day. The rest of the day the teen spends texting, tweeting, sharing photos, and chatting in video chat rooms and online apps. Then there is school, sports, DVDs, TV, movies, music, friends and online games. All too often, parents use technology as a convenient babysitter.

Technology is a beautiful thing. It connects. It creates. It opens doors never before possible. That is good. Today our children have access to more knowledge than any other generation in history.

However, *access* is a two-way street. The Internet is uncharted territory with few rules. The World Wide Web opens the door to worlds that no culture, no generation, no one on the face of the earth is prepared for. Normally a young person learns about the specifics of danger from the parent. However, most parents grew up without the Internet and they don't recognize the specific dangers themselves. The dialogue between parent and child has decreased and outside influence has increased exponentially. Even face time between parent and child often degenerates to clipped syllables sandwiched between texts and tweets. So that begs the question: "Who's grooming our children?"

This book is *not* an Internet safety instruction book. Indeed, there are hundreds of Internet safety programs that are excellent tools for both parents and children. *Seduced* is all about how *access* is used to *groom and recruit* young people, which all too often ends in *exploitation*. It is designed to be a parent-empowering program. It is a guide for parents to understand the influence and coercion processes, and most critically, equip adults with dialogue, insights and psychology that can put the power back into parenting. In essence, it is understanding the psychology behind technology. It is about unprecedented access to groom a child's soul.

To address this issue, it is imperative that we take an honest look at how technology can groom and seduce unsuspecting young people, even while the parent is watching.

In 2011, Shawn Henry, Executive Assistant Director to the FBI, estimated that there are 750,000 child predators online at any given time. Current data is hard to obtain, but all indications are the number easily exceeds one million by 2015. The period of 2012 to 2015 has brought tremendous advances in technology in speed, bandwidth, sophistication of apps, and global user capacity. Nearly every week we hear of a new app or website that will provide our children with Internet video chat rooms that will accommodate up to five hundred people (most are strangers) at any given time.

As I write this there is new technology called PERISCOPE that stands to rock the world of exploitation. It is LIVE STREAMING technology where a teen can video transmit to literally millions of strangers around the globe on their smart phone and it will geo track back to their location. While this will be a great technology bringing the world closer together, it also provides the opportunity for a teenager to reach out to tens of thousands of individuals whose goal is to seduce and exploit them. Please follow Million Kids on Facebook to see how this technology will change our lives.

MMORPGs (massive multi-player online role playing games) are becoming extremely sophisticated, simulating real life experiences and allowing the user to interact with large groups of players while simultaneously providing individual action that often emulates real life circumstances.

In gaming, not only is the access to large groups important, but often they are part of your team, and to be successful you need their approval of your performance. Animation and graphic arts have advanced to the degree that it is often hard to tell animation from real life experiences, and leaves the user alternating between dealing with the challenges of day-to-day living while retreating to the perceived control and euphoria that takes place in a carefully crafted cyber environment. Who wants to deal with laundry, discipline, bill paying, and house cleaning when you can be young, attractive, thin, sexy, smart, and all-powerful in your self-created fantasy world? Trust me, this has not gone unnoticed by predators or marketers.

Think about this. Handing your child a smartphone opens the door to hundreds of thousands of strangers with the ability to write a message on your child's soul. Certainly most will never reach your child, but it only takes one with ill intent and a seductive offer and the appearance of a harmless friendship. Even if a child is not accessed and harmed physically, the breadth of the Internet provides the opportunity to access and groom your child's thinking, create shame and guilt, and influence or prejudice a child's thinking in ways never before conceived. Certainly, there have been vast amounts of outside influence available to a young person for decades, but the difference is that it is not just information being presented. Smartphones open the door for one-on-one conversation with individuals whom a parent would normally never select to groom their child. Even more important, the influence of the parent is diminished as outside influence shapes a young person's ideology.

Let me give you an example. As I write this, yet another American teenager has been accessed, brainwashed, and recruited to join ISIS to fight in Syria. In a different case, twenty year old Christopher Cornell from Ohio was arrested for threatening to detonate a pipe bomb on national landmarks after proclaiming his allegiance to ISIS. In a television interview his mother and grandfather said they were astonished. They stated that Chris was the last person they would have suspected because he was such a nice kid who just played video games several hours a day. My guess is that these fine folks did not realize that many video games come with chat rooms and subgroups of chat rooms where young people can be influenced and groomed by total strangers while competing in a fantasy state. This environment creates an incubator for grooming a person's views on morality, spirituality, sexuality and yes, even political inclinations. Hopefully this is an extreme example, but I believe it is fair.

Four years ago, it would have been much harder for ISIS to even access U.S. teens. Today, technology has provided them with access to millions of teens to target with 24/7 interactions. Grooming is subtle and never recognized by parents in the early stages. The teen is intrigued by a website or meets someone in a video chat room. Perhaps they are captivated by a concept and they surf the web, finding enticing arguments about how America is the great Satan. It could start with a hash tag tweet that gets their attention. Initially, it is like sticking a toe in the water, but the door is open for dialogue. Secret friendships build. They text, they tweet, and become intrigued. They begin to perceive themselves as a cool radical going against the mainstream. ISIS begins to make them prove their loyalty. Confidentiality is key to proving their friendship. They are being sucked in. It is called grooming.

They begin to explore the idea that America is the aggressor and has committed great sins and that most people in America are Imperialist pigs. (Note: this is *their* position, not mine.)

Here is my point: This is a conversation that should be taking place been parent and teen. But the parents are oblivious because the conversation is taking place right in front of them but in secret. The parents do not recognize what they are observing. They sense a change in their teen but can't put their hands on what is truly happening, until one day there is a crisis.

Parents normally influence a teen's perception of right and wrong, the history of sacrifice for our country, and concepts of the price of freedom and the pride that comes with patriotism. Parents would normally dialogue with their teen about the importance of spiritual concepts like knowing God and spiritual perspectives of war and concepts of good versus evil. Without outside influence, I doubt that most teens would ever be drawn into ISIS. Today, the news media is full of stories of young people from around the globe being accessed, groomed, and recruited into ISIS. Teens from the U.K., France, Canada, and the U.S. are shown on the nightly news. Often there is a perplexed parent trying to explain how it happened when they are not sure themselves.

Without contest, I would agree that teens have been going off the grid for years. It is part of the rebellion of teen development as young people try out new ideologies and decide they want to take some radical position to establish their independence and identity. The "hippie" movement of the 60s is the stereotype of an era of rebellion. However, there is a critical difference. The parent usually could observe what was going on and offer a counter point of view, even if it fell on deaf ears. Today, grooming is like a silent cancer metastasizing in front of the parent without a conscious realization or recognition of what is happening.

Let me suggest a more common and less dramatic scenario. A fifteen-year-old girl learns she is pregnant. The boyfriend appears to be wavering in his support.

She is terrified that if mom and dad find out, they will throw her out. She knows she will be ostracized at school. She doesn't want an abortion, but she doesn't want a baby either. She Googles "abortion". She goes on the Planned Parenthood website. They make it sound like it is no big deal. A couple of hours and it is over and no one has to know. In her state, she does not even need her parents' consent.

She is a Christian. She believes abortion is wrong. However, they provide her with an online counselor who reassures her that everyone is doing this. She texts a couple of friends. One confides she had an abortion last year. An online pharmacy picks up the inquiry from the Planned Parenthood database and they start sending her ads about the morning after pill. She wonders if it is too late. She begins to get birth control offers for "afterward."

This scenario is not all that uncommon. What is missing here is that in the past, the dialogue would have started between mother and daughter, and the mother would have been able to share her wisdom. All too often now, the parent either never learns of the situation or only learns of it much later. Outsiders have driven the teen's decision processes.

Let's look at another example. A fourteen-year-old guy is playing a game on X-Box or PlayStation. A "girl" becomes his friend. They flirt and the relationship advances to intimate talk. She wants a photo. He is in heat. Stupidly, he takes a "selfie" in all of his naked glory and sends it off.

It turns out the "girl" is a fifty-nine-year-old male pedophile from Nevada who begins to blackmail him, making threats to expose him, humiliate him in front of friends and family, and destroy him at school if he does not send more photos or meet up with him for sex. Who can he tell? He is terrified, humiliated, and begins to berate himself emotionally. He is ruined forever. He feels shame and guilt. He cannot sleep. He starts to question his sexuality. He wonders if maybe he is homosexual. He is afraid to go to school, because what if the photo turns up on Facebook or Instagram?

He has not been sexually violated. Few would disagree that his self-esteem, his self-worth, his self-respect have been exploited, and he begins to see himself in a "damaged goods" trap.

Predators never look like we think they do. Sometimes they are peers. Sometimes it is a girl, or a dirty old man pretending to be a girl, or a pimp pretending to be a boyfriend, or a bottom girl (aka, girl recruiting for a pimp) looking to lure a young girl into prostitution. The more apps and websites teens access, the more likely they are to be targeted. Sites like Omegle boast a slogan: "Talk with Strangers." Children today surf from app to app with the intent of "hooking up." A Pew poll recently suggested that eighty-seven percent of teens sleep with their phones. Why? They want to be accessed. They are looking to be needed. They are seeking approval and instant gratification and recognition. In this case, access equals vulnerability.

CHAPTER ONE

THE *E-CHASM*

As a lecturer and speaker on issues of human trafficking and teen exploitation, I often conduct training programs for both parents and teens across the U.S. These encounters keep me current on trends in teen app/cell phone use and challenges for parents in trying to raise responsible children and keep them safe from predators. Recently, I spoke at a church in Clovis, California that was a quite enlightening. The parents happened to all sit on one side of the room and the teens on the other. I asked the parents to share the most common websites and apps they use. The answer was typical: Facebook and Instagram. A couple of them played Farmville. One played Candy Crush.

When I asked the teens to name their favorite apps and websites, it was a real eye-opener. The answers were: Kik, Omegle, ooVoo, Snapchat, Poof, Yik Yak, etc. As I stood in the room, I realized that we are facing a true e-chasm (or an electronic chasm) between parent and child.

Think of this. We have a generation of young people who have never *not* known the Internet. We have generations of parents and grandparents who are techno-phobic and some are techno-impotent. It is indeed the great divide. Without the knowledge of how dangerous websites can provide access to and grooming of a child, a parent is nearly impotent.

Recently, I spent time with a father of a four-teen-year-old daughter, a beautiful girl from a solid family. They were poor and the family had never owned a computer. The father wanted his daughter to be like her friends, so he worked overtime to save the money to buy his daughter a smartphone. Right in front of his eyes, in his own home, the girl went on Kik, a sexting and hookup app used by over 200 million users (more than half are minors), and there she met a guy who said he was nineteen. The young lady later became angry with her parents (as will eventually happen with all fourteen-year-olds) and snuck out to the mall and met up with the Kik boyfriend. He was a pimp. He forced her into prostitution and sex trafficked her all over Southern

California with the Crips gang. She and her family were devastated.

The family spent weeks with law enforcement, looking for their daughter. I will never forget the tears pouring from the father's eyes as he said, "I'm her father. I am supposed to protect her. I never knew what Kik was or how it worked. I gave her that phone and now I have lost my daughter."

Eventually the daughter was found by law enforcement and now she is back with her family, getting counseling and medical help, but her life will never be the same. All it took was one app, one encounter, and her life and the life of her family was altered forever.

It occurred to me as I stood facing the *e-chasm* before me that never before in our lifetime, perhaps never before in history, has there been such a challenge to parenting. Historically, down through the ages, parenting was based on the parent's own life experience. Famous lines have developed such as: "Because I am the mom, that's why." "It is 'No' because dad said it was 'No,' so don't argue with me."

Especially in America, the twenty-first century trend has been based on raising "happy" children. Indulging children to have what the parents were not able to have as children appears not only desirable, but rather is a statement of the parent's own commercial success. In most homes, parents made the final decisions as to what the family watched on television, what the child ate, and determined the appropriate friends and play activities for their child. Certainly as more and more households became two-parent working households, children inherently received more latitude in decision making and spent more time away from the parents, lessening their parental impact. Then came massive multi-channel television with an ever-broadening range of edgy stories exploring the outer limits of appropriate sex and violence. Next was reality TV, rock and rap music, and TV icons and teenage idols, including Britney Spears, Snoop Dog, KISS, Madonna, Miley Cyrus and Rihanna. With each new edgy performance, we gradually changed the standards of what is acceptable to the public and redefined our moral compasses. Still, the parent could view the content of the various media together with their family and make parental decisions for appropriateness or at the very least guide the dialogue about various issues in questionable content such as sexuality, abortion, straight versus gay, etc.

A friend of mine often says, "Yesterday's porn is today's norm." It sometimes appears like morality and good taste have been sacrificed on the altar of art and freedom of expression. Just because we can does not mean we should. Just because it is out there does not mean it is always wise to try it. Just because it is free does not mean it is harmless to your child's soul.

The challenge in today's technological world is that the parent is often uninformed and oblivious to the fantasy world the child is maneuvering through right in their own living room, at their dining table, or in the back seat of their car. Even if they are able to perceive and understand what their child is viewing, they are either incapable or unwilling to explore the impact each encounter has on grooming their child's sense of right and wrong, truth and personal decency. They are still the parent, but without knowledge and engagement the parent is powerless. Parents may be even less conscious of the emotional impact on their child as they engage in Internet relationships, access edgy websites, or maybe desperately seeking approval of an online boyfriend or fellow player in their gaming guild. Most parents are woefully ill-equipped to understand the emotional roller coasters their child is experiencing in the cyber world, as well as the psychological needs and desires they are seeking to fulfill through their cyber friends.

CHAPTER TWO

DIGITAL GROOMING

I n some ways young people are already groomed through technology. Look around when you go to the mall, the market, airports, and restaurants. Everyone who has thirty seconds of free time plays with their phone. That is true of adults as well as young people. Most people take their phone to the bathroom with them, and it is believed that as many as twenty percent of phone users have lost it in the toilet. (I am one of them.) So parents are giving their stamp of approval to obsessive teen cell phone use simply by example.

In conversations with Riverside Police Chief Sergio Diaz, we realized that there is a trend he calls "digital narcissism". I concur that this is an accurate description. You see it all the time. You are trying to talk to another person and they get a text, a tweet, or they have to check their email, and then sometimes they have to answer while you are speaking with them. Getting employees to shut off their phone in a meeting is like pulling teeth.

Sometimes you see people checking their phones during the sermon at church. We all are aware of the dangers of texting and driving. Most parents tell their children to get off the phone and talk with them during dinner, and then the parent gets a text, but it is "different" because it is from work. Parents lead by example.

I believe "digital narcissism" accurately identifies this activity. In reality, this person is saying to you that whatever is going on in his/her world is a lot more important than you and what is happening in your world. Let's examine what is behind this.

Have you ever left your phone behind or forgotten your iPad? How did you deal with that? I haven't met you, but I already know the answer. You went nuts. You had internal panic. You felt lost. You couldn't focus on other problems because you were agitated. You were frustrated. You were bored. You were afraid you were missing something. You couldn't check the news. You didn't know what time it was. "Did I have an appointment later?" Even when driving, you know better, but you check your phone when you come to a red light. You send a text in the bathroom.

The addiction aspect of cell phone usage is a fascinating study. One does not need a formal research project to make common observations. Have you ever been on an elevator or in a parking lot or the waiting line of a bank lobby and *not* seen people on their cell phones? It is difficult to understand the issue in totality. Perhaps we all just want to be important, maybe thinking someone would actually value our opinion. We all like to be needed, loved, and sought out. Maybe it is a desire to have external circumstances lift our mood or change our luck or improve our outlook for the day. Maybe most of us are lonely and want to be valued, and with each check of an email we improve our odds. Perhaps we are addicted to outside stimulation and having others be responsible for keeping us motivated and upbeat. Perhaps it is fear of bad news, and as long as there are no emails or texts, we can feel safe. Whatever the truth is, few would argue that our society has become addicted to technology.

I believe I would be remiss if I failed to explore an inconvenient truth. Many adults enjoy escaping into the cyber world themselves. Many parents look the other way at their teen's addiction because it keeps the teen busy and provides more time for the adults to enjoy their own lives. Most parents are as addicted to their smartphones as their teens are. The thought of putting their phone away for one or two hours at a time is extremely threatening to them. So their very behavior puts the parental stamp of approval on the teen's addictive behavior. Most parents live busy lives and they justify allowing their teen on apps, games etc., so they themselves will not have to take time out of their lives to interact with their child. Some parents (especially men) are as addicted to video gaming as their children, and therefore justify it as having a shared interest.

A slippery slope is that many men (dads) are also addicted to online porn. Sometimes the porn is in the games. Most men believe their children should not be exposed to porn, but never stop themselves. Most of those same parents do not play the games *with* their teen. Some parents are addicted to living in sound bites and therefore rationalize to themselves that it is okay for their children to spend nine hours a day on the Internet because everyone is doing it. They rationalize, "You just can't fight it anymore."

I find this an interesting phenomenon. It is the convenient justification for the activities they really want to pursue that trump parenting. They are not bad parents, but they are living on the edge. A successful businessman or woman will think nothing of leaving their fourteen-year-old son or daughter to play games or video chat for the afternoon, and refuse to look at the reality of their teen's activities. They soothe their consciences by saying, "He is nearly an adult. Besides I am his Facebook friend." These are the same parents who would never leave their son or daughter off at a porn bar or strip club just to keep him busy until they get home from work.

However, millions of parents are doing that each day without admitting that some of the people on the Internet would like to have sex with their son or daughter. Many predators are looking to groom and recruit your child so they can sell them into prostitution and sex slavery. I know because I talk with these children and parents regularly. They would have never believed that they would find themselves and their teens caught in a web of deceit. They reassure themselves that their children are responsible and will exercise good judgment. Yet, still they have no dialogue. They never take a second look. They do not sit with their teen and understand their avatar. They do not look at the websites they are exploring and talk with their child about what they learned. Sometimes gaming and the Internet are convenient babysitters. They are busy.

A couple of surveys conducted in 2013 showed that twenty percent of U.S. adults admitted to checking their smartphone during sex, and in the U.K., sixty percent of women admitted to checking their smartphones during sex. Okay, I cannot resist. If checking a smartphone is more important than getting laid, do we think we might have an *obsession* here?

Talk about being "groomed". We are like rats in a maze. We might need to rearrange Maslow's hierarchy of needs. Smartphones might be right up there with food and shelter. Truthfully, we are a society addicted. We are a society obsessed. We try discipline, but we find ourselves making excuses to use it again. My guess is that using discipline and breaking habits involving smartphones will be more difficult than dieting or stopping smoking or biting your nails. The need to be needed and valued by others may be the biggest addiction for every one of us. Psychologists will tell you that you cannot break an addiction with discipline. That is why Alcoholics Anonymous works. Willpower will not break an addiction. Obsessions are even more complex. Obsessions are based on internal fantasy and convenient beliefs. An obsessed person will go to great lengths to justify their behavior. I contend that most of us around the globe are obsessed with smartphone usage and the need to be needed. Digital narcissism is a true obsession.

Please stop with me as you read this book and think this through and through. What does that mean when you hand your kid a smartphone?

I think this might be one of the most important concepts that need to be researched in the twenty-first century. Think about children who are eleven, twelve, thirteen, or even fourteen years old. They are going through puberty. They are hormonal. Their frontal lobes will not be fully developed for several years. They are exploring who they are and are trying to be independent, while still needing the reassurances that come with dependence. Their cognitive reasoning is just starting to develop. We hand them a smartphone. It is literally a highway to digital heaven or digital hell, depending on how they choose to use it. We give them all kinds of lectures. Do not sext. Do not talk to strangers. Do not send naked photos. Do not go on porn sites. If you break the rules, I will take your phone from you. I am going to check your phone regularly. Do not use it at school. Don't send over one hundred texts a day. Be careful who you talk to, etc.

What we are saying to them is this: "Even though I am obsessed and even though I am addicted, it is okay because I am an adult. I am your parent. I expect you to use this phone and not be obsessed and not be addicted. You are a child and I don't want you in danger, so I expect you to show discipline in usage, even if I do not."

So we discipline them, even when we do not discipline ourselves. When they violate the rules, like going on a porn site, we are surprised that our responsible kid would do such a thing and respond with lectures and grounding them.

Don't get me wrong. I am absolutely in favor of setting rules and enforcing consequences. A twelve-year-old who is caught sexting to a twenty-five-year-old needs to have the phone removed until they can understand the dangers of their actions. My point here is that *before* you give a kid a smartphone, you need to have a clear understanding of the total environment your teen is dealing with once you hand them the keys to the kingdom. You are the parent. You are most likely paying for this device.

Later in this book, we will deal with the psychological impact of a young person being seduced, and how to deal with it. Right now, I hope to open your eyes to the true reality of smartphone usage for both parents and teens, and how to talk about it. The bottom line is that both adults and teens will react the same way. They will become digital narcissists. As an adult, you have the cognitive reasoning skills to recognize spam, an illicit offer, or a smooth-talking guy or girl looking to hook up with no strings attached. You know that an ad for "lonely housewives" is not an ad for maid service. And a chance to go "around the world" is not a solicitation for a travel agency.

To understand just how much our world has changed in the past five years, and also how critical it is to recognize these trends and adjust our parenting techniques, let me share the results from a couple of polls about Internet usage. These polls are from Pew Research and Piper Jaffrey.

- Ninety-five percent of teens are online. Ninety percent of online teens use some kind of social media.
- Seventy-six percent of teens are on Instagram and fifty-nine percent of teens use Twitter.
- Facebook (which most parents monitor) has dropped to only forty-five percent used by teens.
- Eighty-seven percent of teens text message at least occasionally. On average eighteen-to-twenty-four-year-olds send 130 texts a day or 3,853 a month.
- Eighty-three percent of teens report using their phones to take pictures and sixty-four percent of teens share pictures with others.

- Ninety-one percent post a photo of themselves (as of 2012), up from seventy-nine percent in 2006.
- Thirty-two percent of teens exchange videos on their phones (Pew). This is fast increasing with Internet speed and capacity expansions.

Equally important as examining trends in cell phone and Internet usage is the amount of information that teens are willing to reveal about themselves to strangers. This is an important trend in understanding the concept of a predator accessing and grooming a young person, and how they use the data to decide who will be the easiest target to pursue.

According to a 2012 *Pew Research Poll* regarding sites with profiles:

- Seventy-one percent of teens post their school name.
- Seventy-two percent post the city or town where they live.
- Ninety-two percent post their real name to the profile.
- Eighty-four percent post their interests such as movies, music, books.

- Eighty-two percent post their birth date – a real billboard for predators looking to hook up with minors.
- Sixty-two percent post their relationship status.
- Ninety-one percent post a photo of themselves.
- Twenty-four percent post videos of themselves.

Keeping current on changing trends and maintaining accurate latest data is a full-time enterprise. Many of these figures are most likely changing, considering that these figures are the latest obtainable on the Internet. There have been significant technological advancements, apps, animation, video production, and expansion of capacity, opening the door to large-scale video chat rooms and technologies like the "look around" button that allows the user to identify potential new "friends" based on GPS and your current location.

In October of 2014, Piper Jaffray, an investment bank and asset management firm, released some new research data that suggests that Instagram and Twitter have surpassed Facebook for usage by teenagers. It is important that parents understand this change in website and app usage, because many conscientious parents have become their teens' "friends" on Facebook and believe that monitoring their teens' posts is sufficient to be aware of what the teens are doing online.

As you can see from the stats above, Facebook is declining in popularity as young people turn to Instagram, texting, and Twitter. However, I am still dumbfounded by the number of cases even today where the predators access and groom victims through Facebook.

One of the most concerning statistics published recently stated that more than seventy percent of teens believe that what they do online should be a secret. I find this a fascinating concept, because they are posting all of their life's activities on the *World Wide Web.* Hello! They think their parents should not be privy to the secrets of their lives.

It is my observation, in working with cases of teen recruitment, that teens who are especially putting themselves "out there" to be found by strangers have changed their Internet usage patterns. Parents are happy to post on Facebook and some also post on Instagram. Teens, however, will create multiple accounts and hop back and forth between them. For instance, a teen may have a Kik address, which does not need to be tied to a cell phone number. They meet strangers on Omegle, ooVoo, Vine, and others and then go to Kik to develop the relationship, which sometimes ends as a sexting relationship. Sexting, if you are not aware, is in essence like having virtual sex through cell phone messages as you text out sexually explicit acts, usually to total strangers or strangers who are becoming your new best friend. Teens tell me the raunchier the act and the less you know the person, the more of an adrenaline rush you get. The bottom line is that if a parent is still monitoring a teen's activity on Facebook, they will believe that everything is good and nothing dangerous is taking place. Often they are kidding themselves.

Posting your profile and personal comments on multiple websites and apps brings an additional risk for a young person. Most predators understand the concept of "breadcrumbs." In other words, when teens set up their profiles and post personal posts on multiple apps and sites, they are building a personal image of themselves. They are leaving a trail of clues. Predators understand how this works and will comb through the various profiles as they identify a vulnerable target.

Add to that the fact that many teens think nothing of baring their soul to friends. "I am sad, I broke up with my boyfriend. My dad is traveling again. I can't stand my mom's boyfriend. I am afraid I won't get that job. I am flunking out of that class. I have dieted all week and only lost two pounds." All of these comments will build a profile for a predator. To teenagers, it is just what is going on in their lives. To a predator, it is a roadmap to accessing vulnerable young people and grooming them for control and manipulation.

Let me translate this for you. She is depressed and easily influenced. She is looking to be loved. She does not have a strong man in her life. She is not getting along with her mom. She needs money. She has low self-esteem. She is overweight and feels bad about herself. She is looking for someone to rescue her and make her feel loved and important. He then arranges a video chat room encounter, sends a text, tweet, Instagram post. It is innocent enough. Just a quick little funny thing to get her attention. They text, they tweet, they sext, they send photos, they exchange YouTube videos, and he becomes her knight in shining armor, her new best friend. She is addicted to his approval.

In the work that Million Kids has done with Dr. Andrew Doan, PhD, MD, we have explored the idea of addiction to technology and the role it plays in an addiction to immediate feedback and instant gratification. Some of the findings can be found on his website, realbattle.org. It is our observation (and his are much more scientific than mine) that there are multiple layers of addiction taking place in a teen's addiction to smartphones, apps, social media, and gaming. There is obviously an addiction to being needed. There is an adrenaline addiction, as each interaction has the potential to change your mood. There is an addiction to approval as each encounter just might say something positive and uplifting to you. I think there is also an addiction to "control," in the sense that you are getting constant feedback. That stimulates the need to make certain your life is as you perceive it should be and that no one is presenting outside interference. Make no mistake about it: this is *not* unique to teens. Adults, yes, even the most educated and sophisticated adults, check their smartphones every five minutes. Some may even have a PhD in "Digital Narcissism".

Student Science Magazine conducted research that indicated your average student uses their cell phone for nine hours per day. Truthfully, that could be a good thing as students research answers to assignments, etc. Again, technology has many major advantages if used maturely and in the appropriate setting.

One side trip I often take mentally is how this affects our spirituality and the spiritual leadership for our children. How does one look internally and do self-examination if ninety-nine percent of our day is spent looking externally? The reason this concept is worth exploring, to me, is that it appears our moral compass is determined by: 1) Our inner conscience such as our sense of right and wrong; and 2) Our upbringing by those adults who placed moral guidance in us at a young age.

There are three contributing factors that merit exploration here.

First: If a child or teen has virtually no alone time, how do they learn to explore the depth of their own feelings? If teens have their phones with them ninety percent of a day and eighty-seven percent of teens sleep with their phones, it would appear that right now, more than any time on earth, a young person is looking outward for character development rather than understanding their own internal messaging. They will let a multitude of strangers and marketers set the standards for them. I believe that this is an important, albeit extremely subtle, shift in our society. If the primary feelings being experienced by a young person are reactive or enhanced by melodrama, the teen will never know quality sound confidence within their inner soul. Marketers, gamers, and 24/7 news media tweets are all designed for a person to *react*. Reaction is not feeling, per se. It is important for a person to be able to experience deep introspection to be able to mature and develop depth.

Secondly, spirituality is based on time spent contemplating a higher power, a force greater than yourself. It is important to stop and look around your world and realize that you are but a speck on the universe. I believe it is important to realize that your time on earth is limited and that you have certain gifts and talents that can make the world a better place. Balance comes from understanding that there is a certain rhythm to life. An often-quoted Bible verse comes to mind. "Be still and know that I am God" (Psalm 46:10). It is often the quiet of the morning or the still small voice that guides us to know ourselves and our relationship with God. If young people spend the bulk of their time on elec-tronic devices, they will spend limited time enjoying nature, expending energy, or finding their private thoughts in relationship to a greater world. In virtu-ally all religions of the world, there is an element of meditation. There is a need for contemplation, for centering the soul. It would appear that in this fast-paced, high-tech world with 24/7 interconnection with others, introspection and quiet soul searching might be a lost art.

Finally, without quiet introspection, we are not clear about our own personal identity. It is in these moments that we form concepts, explore possibil-ities, and decide what we stand for. Our days are spent being bombarded by marketers with carefully crafted messages and shielded intents for our lives. If we are sending and receiving 150 texts or tweets a day, then we are allowing a multitude of influences to set the standard for our own acceptance. We begin to doubt ourselves. We begin to think, "Maybe we are not talented after all." We hedge our sense of morality. For example, "Everyone who takes an online test cheats a little." "Cheating online is not really cheating. Having a relationship with another person online when you are committed to a different person is okay because it is not really cheating when nothing physical has happened. We are just sexting." We will explore more about this in the next chapter, Digital Morality.

It is my perception that the Internet brings with it a parallel universe where reality is not applicable because the Internet is not real life. We rationalize we can live with one set of morals online and expect young people to live by a higher standard in real life. True spirituality grows out of a sense of who you are in relationship to right and wrong, truth or lies, cowardice or valor, giving and taking. Building strong self-worth and developing character comes from knowing who you are and what you stand for. That takes time spent in introspection and gaining knowledge and building principles that represent you as the valuable person you are. It is doubtful this would ever take place in eight hours of video gaming.

What a great opportunity this provides for the savvy parent or grandparent. It is critical that adults understand the concept of what is happening and take constructive, deliberate measures to be spiritual leaders for our young people. I encourage you to learn the terms and set time aside with your young person and dialogue. Certainly it may be awkward at first, but it is well worth the effort. If they won't put the game away or put the smartphone down, then use that as the dialogue starter.

If they are gaming, explore with them about the game and talk about how they "feel" about the game. If they say they don't feel, then explore why not. Get them to talk about it. Would they consider doing that in real life? Why not? Why is it okay that they can do that on the Internet, but not in real life? Just because it is a game, is it any less moral? Are they concerned that they don't feel bad committing an act that would make them feel bad if they did it in real life? How does that affect their spirituality? Does it change their relationship with God? What does their avatar stand for? Are they proud of their online persona and reputation? Does their avatar do what is right or just what is easy or whatever is necessary to get points and win? Open the discussion to the concept of winning at all costs. Interesting to me is that we often teach our sons and daughters this concept when they were playing in little league but have given up the effort as they get older. This may be the most critical time in their lives to learn about character as they become young adults.

My greatest concern when it comes to the subject of "grooming" is the vast array of outside influences that can now "groom" a child's mind and soul. This becomes particularly threatening when it is the mind of a young person who is being "groomed." The challenge to parenting is how to guide, mentor, and dialogue with a young person to help them evaluate an unprecedented exposure to others wishing to influence and motivate them into dangerous and destructive avenues. Truly, more than any other time in the history of mankind, outsiders are able to plant ideas into a young person's thinking. The avenues and vehicles are nearly endless.

- Rap songs glorifying pimping and whores, killing, and getting even.
- Social media apps where you have first-person experience with the devil, hanging, masturbation, and experimenting with bi-sexuality.
- Animated pornography is just for fun. It is not really porn.

- ISIS sending out mass propaganda and glorifying the war for Allah.
- Less extreme, but more destructive is the appearance of a new friend who thinks "you're hot" and wants to hook up.

By now, you may begin to think of me as an extremist. Perhaps you think I am a person who sees the boogeyman around every corner. It is simply not true.

Training thousands of people from every walk of life, I see a lot. I know there are many great parents and strong children with good integrity. I can spot a well-trained young person in the first five seconds of a presentation. It is usually easy to tell which child has had a strong upbringing with good role models and involved parents, and those who do not. However, in my line of work I have sat with some of the best parents who are searching for their children because they have been lured into prostitution, or have received an online solicitation, or their child needs to change schools because of a certain naked photo being circulated.

Let me share with you a story I heard from a lady attending a government training I conducted on human trafficking. This woman was about thirty-five and obviously intelligent, and my guess was that she and her husband were conservative Christian parents. She said they had twin eleven-year-old daughters. They were good girls and she felt they had a strong relationship. The girls wanted iPhones for Christmas because everyone else had them. Mom said, "No," but dad said, "Yes." He convinced the mother that the girls were exceptionally responsible for their age and they had never had any trouble with them. The mother capitulated. She stipulated that the phones be checked at any time and that they would read all their emails, texts, and be their friend on Facebook. For the first three or four weeks, she did all that, but parents get busy. One day the Mom borrowed her daughter's phone to take a photo. She thought she saw her daughter flinch. She decided to look through the phone, as she had not checked it for a while. Right before her eyes, it was obvious her eleven-year-old daughter had been sexting to a thirty-five-year-old man in Iowa.

It is cases like these that have driven me to write this book. This could be anybody's daughter or son, and the sexting could have been found "after" he came out to see her. Either way, her normally innocent eleven-year-old girl has learned about puberty from a predator.

One of the greatest changes in the twenty-first century is not only the level of exposure of a young person to thousands of predators, but much more disturbing is the level of exposure teens will knowingly or unknowingly create for themselves. They usually have no concept of the level of danger they are placing themselves in. In some cases, the teen understands the danger and will prefer to walk on the wild side, but they are totally incapable of projecting out the depth of violence and exploitation waiting for them if they make a bad choice. Still, they post a plethora of information on the web, doing their best to look sophisticated and experienced. It is called a "profile."

Many teens are blatant in their posting of personal data. A lesser percent of young people are not only careless in the posting of personal data, but more likely are practically "trolling" for attention. One frustrated mother I sat with exclaimed, "The predator is not chasing her. My daughter is throwing herself out there to see what she can get." Obviously the parent/child relationship was in deep trouble and the teenager had breached all cautions that the parent had provided.

This is an extremely important point in the changing trends of our society. In the past, predators had significant challenges finding a potential victim, accessing them and then grooming them for exploitation. The Internet has changed this dynamic entirely.

To a predator, apps, social media, and gaming are a virtual candy store.

An unsupervised or out-of-control young person can find a new friend in a matter of minutes by posting provocative photos or making suggestions of availability. The Internet is like a global version of a bathroom wall (graffiti). "For a good time call XXXXX." All you have to do is go onto YouTube and look at several uploads from Omegle, ooVoo and Chatroulette. Certainly most parents would find solace in the fact that their child would not do this. Interestingly enough, there is no shortage of teens creating a global advertisement of their availability, and the raunchier the better. Surely the greater percentage of these teens are not orphans. Somewhere there are parents who would be appalled if they took the time to understand the path these young people have chosen and the danger they are placing themselves in.

The availability and expansion of video chat rooms will bring a whole new level of opportunity for those young people who are promiscuous and choose to throw caution to the wind. There appears to be a disturbing trend of vulgarity, manipulation, bullying, degrading humor and depravity in first person encounters of teens looking to "hook up." There appears to be no limit to the level of degradation these teens will go to so they will stand out from the crowd or get the attention of fellow trollers. In the U.K., *Newsbeat* published a poll that stated one in three fifteen to eighteen-year-olds have met someone in person they originally met through social media.

In researching these trends, a rational, mature person cannot help but be disturbed. A great deal of research needs to take place to understand how widespread this "hook up" mentality permeates the average teen thinking. Speculation could run the entire gamut. Perhaps this is providing an accelerated vehicle for those street children, delinquent and at-risk children to express themselves and link up with other children who prefer to go "off the grid" morally and spiritually. The availability of video chat room recordings on YouTube gives us extensive insight into how depraved the out-of-control person can be on the Internet. Rather than cream rising to the top, with the advanced use of technology to enhance talents and capabilities and build strong leaders, these chat rooms are like adding maggots to milk. After watching a few of these encounters, one desires to race out and take a bath.

When you hand a smartphone to a pubescent twelve-year-old, you are opening the door for global input from thousands of people you will never meet. The child will spend more time with their Internet friends than they will with you. *This will mold their thinking.* There is no training tutorial. It is pure trial and error and input from their friends. Most parents are naïve to the dangers of the world of apps, video chat rooms, live streaming and online gaming, and so we have just handed them the keys to a digital vehicle with absolutely no instructions, except, "Be careful, and I will tell you when you break the rules when I catch you." We expect them to not become addicted to being needed or obsessed with experiencing the approval that comes with winning an online game or being admired through a post on Instagram or Facebook. It never occurs to us that sexting is a form of reinforced approval, and pornography on the Internet is not like a *Sports Illustrated* swimsuit calendar. Somehow we think *our child* will be the exception to the rule.

It is my observation that today, many people are handing a ten-year-old a smartphone and they have not even yet had "the talk" (about sex) with their child. Apparently they think it is okay for some guy in Romania to teach them while they are playing a video game. There is some sort of mirage, a false hope on the part of the parents that their child is a good kid and smarter than the average child and so they hope against hope that it will all turn out okay. After all, everybody is doing it.

Let me set the record straight. I do not think that most parents are bad parents. To the contrary most parents are concerned but fearful and in despair as they watch the dynamics of online influence for their child. Many parents express to me that they feel impotent and are frustrated by their lack of ability to get through to their child. Truthfully, it is totally overwhelming even for the most concerned and engaged parent.

Here is the challenge. We have already determined that smartphone usage is an addiction, and in most cases an obsession with most people. Your child will not be the exception. So get ready for it. There are no easy answers, but I believe the bottom line is to use the smartphone to build dialogue and training with your child every day. Spend time talking to your teen about it. Take the secrecy out of it. Ask what apps other children are using. Look at them together. What is wrong or right with these apps? Do they support our moral standards? What are the dangers of that app? Get involved. This exercise is two-fold. It will bring you (as the parent) into the fold. You are no longer techno-phobic or techno-ignorant. Your child will recognize and know that you care enough to learn.

A consistent, non-accusatory dialogue allows you, the parent, the power to explore the concepts of real world morality and not be compromised by digital morality (next chapter). You and your teen are engaged, and you, the parent, can guide the moral, spiritual, and sexual beliefs that are important in the parenting of a child.

Digital grooming is truly a twenty-first century phenomenon. As a standalone factor in societal trends, it has the potential for being a cataclysmic issue. Add to that substantiating and enhancing issues of outside influences and expanding variety fringe groups seeking to influence young people, and this issue may be one of the greatest threats to the family and child safety of our lifetime, but it does not have to be. It is critical to educate the parents and grandparents and put the power back into parenting. Exploitation is not inevitable. Education is the key. That is the goal of this book.

CHAPTER THREE

DIGITAL MORALITY – A PARALLEL UNIVERSE

Killing is not killing. Sex is not sex. Animated pornography is considered art. Because it is not real. Digital morality has no consequences. At least that this *their* story, and they are sticking to it.

As a trainer for law enforcement, I often make presentations about sex trafficking and exploitation to high school students in the U.S. The goal is to help young people understand how predators identify vulnerable teens, groom them, recruit them and exploit them through prostitution, blackmail, sextortion, and child porn rings. Recently I presented to 750 high school students at a conference and *seventy-five percent* of them said they were playing Grand Theft Auto and nearly one-third said they had purchased the recently released GTA V or received it as a gift. In a cursory poll of nearly 2,000 students, GTA is their favorite game, even over World of Warcraft, Clash of the Clans, Minecraft, Black Ops and Call of Duty. GTA V sold over *one billion dollars in games in the first three days* of their release.

The latest release of GTA V features a "first person experience," which is technically possible because of expanded memory capability in computers and bandwidth. In essence it allows the player to experience the event personally as opposed to controlling your avatar as a third party. The promotions suggest it enhances your overall playing experience.

Grand Theft Auto V is notorious because it encourages the player to select and purchase one of three sex acts with a prostitute. This is not a fact to be ignored. The player selects the sex act ($20 for a hand job, $50 for a blow job, $70 for the full sexual act) and pays the price of the service and then suggests that you can beat her up and even kill her so you can get your money back. This act is not mandatory in the video game and by law you have to be eighteen to purchase this game. However, I can tell you in the many presentations that I give in high schools that most students tell me they either already own GTA V or want to purchase it. Virtually all of the students are aware of the prostitute feature of the game.

According to gta.wikia.com in Grand Theft Auto: San Andreas, "If you complete the pimping missions, prostitutes will pay you instead. Different prostitutes with different voices and personalities are featured including possibly a 'crying game' scenario normally after sex." It would appear that we are on the verge of having virtual sex trafficking integrated into a game enjoyed by millions.

Certainly, no one has ever accused GTA developers of using the game to help develop a person's moral compass. The very basics of the game involve killing, bank heists, escapes, torture, melee attacks, explosives, and war is waged against Mexican drug lords, outlaw motorcycle clubs, and Latin American street gangs. As one young man says, "You gotta do what you gotta do to win."

Recently, I was conducting sex trafficking training programs at Pomona High School in California, where several hundred students showed the same excitement about the release of the new GTA V. One bright young man sat on the front row and he was particularly enthusiastic about Grand Theft Auto V. Knowing how GTA works, I couldn't help but ask the obvious questions. I asked him if he had played the part of GTA V that included the prostitute and he laughed and said, "Sure." I asked him how he felt about that. He replied, "What do you mean?"

So I asked him if he felt any guilt. He scoffed and laughed. Fascinated, I asked again to be clear. "So you selected a particular sex act based on price, you pay the prostitute, you have sex with the prostitute, and then you kill her so you don't have to give up your money, and you don't experience anything?"

He laughed and shrugged and said, "It is no big deal. It is just a game. It is what you have to do to win."

There was nothing abnormal about this kid. He appeared like anybody's son. Just doing what you have to do to win.

Think about this encounter. This young man is telling me it's okay to maim, kill, and brutalize hundreds of animated people, in fact it is desirable so he gets the most points. His approval from his guild depends on his effectiveness in violence. It is okay because there are no real life consequences to his decision. In fact, there *are* consequences if he does not kill because he experiences the rejection of his guild. These actions are mandatory or you will be exiled from your guild.

It is also okay to select a sex act with a prostitute and kill her to get your money back because it is just a game. Again, this young man is trying to convince me that sex is not *real* sex, killing is not *real* killing and *sin on the Internet is not real sin.*

We are teaching our children to make decisions and seek approval in an environment where there are no real life consequences for their actions.

So when is a *game not a game?*

The answer: when it is attached to a chat room with groups and subgroups to mold a player's thinking – for starters. When violence and violation are essential to succeed. When animated sex can develop into hard-core pornography addiction. When total strangers infiltrate your child's thinking and get them to believe that God will not count Internet sin as sin.

This venue is teaching our children that we have the right to rewrite the words of God. As long as it is animated, as long as it is just an electronic fantasy, we will not be held accountable.

How do we teach a child to glorify God when they are developing into adults in a fantasy world of sorcery, prostitution, violence, and allowing outsiders to write on our children's soul?

These games are designed to be full of intrigue, competition for a high score and acceptance by your team players, accompanied by rap and high impact music to increase the adrenaline and make the gaming experience all-encompassing. Think about the impact on a young person in daily life. Mom says, "Clean up your room," and, "Don't lie to me," and in their pockets is a fantasy world on a smartphone where anything goes. It is my observation that your average twelve-year-old child is not capable of taking the high road. Indeed, I know many twenty-one-year-olds who have not matured enough to sort through real life values and digital morality in a fantasy world.

At this point, I would like to stop and share with you, the reader, my thinking about online gaming and MMORPGs like World of Warcraft, Minecraft, Black Ops and Grand Theft Auto. These are the most well known, but there is an endless variety of game themes and choices for PlayStation and X-Box, some of which get extremely violent and pornographic.

My position is not so much that I am against a teen playing appropriate electronic games, as much as I think it is critical that the parent understand the consequences of their decision to allow their child to participate. It is my observation that this is somewhat of a casual decision on the part of most parents. Most parents have no idea what they are agreeing to expose their child to when they purchase the game. "The child wants it, everyone else has it, and I don't want my child to be considered weird." I find that reasoning sad.

Certainly there are many good features about some of these games. Playing develops hand-eye coordination, expands the vocabulary, perhaps helps with learning history, maybe improves math as gamers calculate stats, etc. It can even open their world up to a whole new group of friends, many of whom will share maturity and insights the teen will not get anywhere else. But the parent should know that the wrong games and the wrong chat rooms can open up a world of violence and vivid depictions of evil, pornography, magic, wizardry, and sorcery. More important, gaming chat rooms open the door to hundreds of individuals to talk to your child in a fantasy state. I would suggest that most parents would never invite many of these individuals into your living room if you met them standing at your front door. Somehow, to a parent, they are not real on the Internet.

In addition to the desensitizing nature of many video games, I am equally concerned about the element of chat rooms. There are sub-groups where the servers are flagged for role playing, seeking the emotional thrill of a fantasy relationship or sexual pleasure in explicit interactions with other players, setting up a person to be accessed, groomed, and exploited. Some sub groups are vile and sadistic. Some have political motivations like ISIS. Some specialize in pornography. Many will interact on a daily basis with your teen. Never before in history have so many specialty perversions had so much access to the average child.

My advice is that if your teen is already playing the game or is nagging you to buy a game, you approach this as a case study with your child. Sit with them. Get them to show you the game and how it works. Talk about what you see in the game in a non-judgmental way. If they have a friend who plays, ask if the two of you can come over and watch them play. Make it a dialogue. Equip yourself to have a reasonable conversation by getting them to share with you. The idea is to take the secrecy out of a world where you have no knowledge or input, instead making it an experience where you can teach your child real life lessons.

Look at the various images on the game and talk about mystical and occult worlds. Are they fantasy or do they really exist? Do some impact on your senses as appearing more evil than others? Certainly in most games, the goal is for the player to overcome evil. Talk about that with your teen. Do they believe there is evil in real life? How is it overcome? Develop a dialogue about war in real life and compare that to war in gaming. Use it as a chance to dialogue and open doors for discussion. What about how law enforcement is treated? How would they feel if that happened in real life? Talk about building character. After all, in gaming you have an avatar and you decide what each stands for. How does that relate to the character your child is building? What values are important to them?

Gamers have a tendency to disappear in a game and shut the world out. Is that what you want for your children? Many give up sports and friends and spend literally hours in gaming, challenged by the need to win and cultivating a belief that this is what they do better than anything else. Parents, I think it is important to not overlook this point. Many children who are considered social nerds disappear into the world of gaming.

An hour or two a day might be educational and helpful to socially backward children, but all too often, the teen will quit trying to find ways to fit into real life. Many of these children will become addicted because they feel safe and comfortable in a fantasy world that they control. Soon their real life world becomes small and they will retreat into a world where they feel they excel. These children are especially vulnerable to being accessed, groomed, and recruited by predators. Often men pretend to be girls and will entice the teen into a fantasy relationship or sharing an illicit photo. The child is quickly sucked in. This is an important discussion to have with a young person if you observe this trend taking place.

In these situations, the parent is going to have to be the strong leader. Get your children away from the computer. Engage in other activities. Recognize their insecurities and encourage success in other activities. However, it takes an informed, caring, and committed parent to understand the issue and implement the changes. You may want to consider purchasing Dr. Andrew Doan's book *Hooked on Games* to learn the more about how to help your teen break the addiction.

If parents are going to allow a game to educate and influence their children, I believe it is their responsibility to make sure that game is going to teach them the moral standards that are healthy for young people. Get engaged with your teen. Educate yourself and take the secrecy out of the gaming world. Make sure the decision you have made will, in fact, make your child a better person. If all of this sounds like too much effort for you as a parent, then don't buy the game. Parents who use MMORPGs for babysitters are literally abandoning their responsibility for parenting and are setting up their children to be accessed, groomed, and recruited by individuals they would never allow in their home.

More research needs to be done to totally understand the psychological impact on players as they maneuver through the maze of ethical decisions within any video game that are essential to winning the game. However, at the very least, it is my observation that there is a "conditioning process" taking place within our society and focused heavily on our youth. Indeed, most families that profess "Christian values" have succumbed to the onslaught of vulgarity, violence, nudity, raucous rap music, and salacious video games to some degree. It is nearly impossible to drive down the street without seeing nudity on billboards, promotions for abortions, ads hailing the latest "most violent movie ever", and a daily offering of sexting and pornography and ads on TV for housewives who want to "hook up." At some point, even your most conscientious parent feels they have to pick and choose their battles.

Certainly the deterioration of morality in media offerings and advertising has progressed for decades. Starting after World War II, and the influx of television, much has been written and presented about introducing violence and sexuality in the home. Most adults were able to view the shows, deciding for ourselves to choose the high road. We recognized that violence and sexuality were just part of a story line and something *others* did, but we chose to live moral and decent lives. The 60s brought a massive shift in our society as drugs were widely available and the "hippie" society appeared to separate the responsible and the dropouts. Movies and television shows have become increasingly violent and sexually explicit, and we all appear to have "adapted."

As we have entered into the twenty-first century, abortions are approved and readily available, in some states without parental consent for minors. Pot (marijuana) is considered a medical remedy, and artists like Miley Cyrus, Madonna, and Rihanna have pushed the boundaries of art versus immorality. Most "Christians" shake their heads, do their best to soldier on, establish their own standards and try to raise their family with old-fashioned values and do what is right in "the sight of the Lord."

However, I would argue that we have crossed a whole new threshold related to what I call the *e-chasm*. For the first time in history, we have children who live in a digital world and we have parents and grandparents who have virtually no understanding of what is being offered to their child. They purchase smartphones for the ten-year-old and say, "Be careful," without truly understanding the consequences of their actions. They soothe their consciences by saying, "He/she is a responsible child and I will monitor what they do," except they are techno-phobic and techno-ignorant. They don't even know what they are looking at when they check a child's phone.

For many parents, handing a ten-year-old a smartphone is like handing a child a grenade and saying, "I have to run to the store, I will be right back. Don't pull that pin, okay?" Most parents are stuck in the, "Because I am the mom and I said no" mentality. In cyberspace, their total experience is limited to Facebook and Instagram. Most parents are cyber-impotent.

They don't want their child to be the only one on the block without a smartphone, and so they capitulate, and they pray they can stay close to their kid and nothing bad will happen. Apps, social media, and gaming are changing our society dramatically, but the change is ever so subtle. It is kind of like seething fog seeping up from the ground below us. The scenario reminds me of the analogy of putting a frog in boiling water. You place a frog in a pot of boiling water; it will either jump out or die immediately. However, if you place a frog in a pot of cold water and heat it up slowly, it will do the backstroke as it is being conditioned to the warming water, until it quietly boils to death.

It is my experience, in working with many of the young people to caution them about becoming victims of child sex trafficking or exploitation, that there is a clear and critical difference in the violence and sexuality experienced in movies and television and the apps, social media, and gaming of this generation. Movies are one way. You view and you go home. The Internet provides *interaction*. Your teen can meet others and others can meet your teen. With each encounter comes influence. Sometimes influence results in action.

We are truly at a unique time in history. More than ever before in our lifetime, children and teens are exposed to hundreds of thousands, if not millions of predators. Many apps and social media sites open up the doors to literally millions of outsiders. We used to tell children, "Don't take candy from strangers." Now we buy them the vehicle that opens the door to strangers, and hope and pray they will recognize candy when they see it, but they won't. It is called "grooming." I know. In my line of work, I sit with heartbroken parents looking for their missing children. I get calls from teens asking me if I can help them get their naked photo back. I look for missing teens that are being sex trafficked on backpage.com or Craig's List, all because they "hooked up" with the wrong "friend."

The latest apps like We Chat have over 450 million users, and actually boast of a "look around" button. Many new apps are based on GPS. A despondent teen that is mad at mom can go to the mall and hit the "look around" button, and it will show them all the people in a one-and-a-half-mile radius who wants to hook up with a stranger. Even more concerning is We Chat allows total anonymity in their user base and has no age restrictions. From a law enforcement perspective, We Chat servers are outside the U.S. and although they state that they respond to law enforcement inquiries they are located in Hong Kong making legal inquiries more time consuming and cumbersome. This can make it more challenging to find and prosecute preda-tors. This is also true of the teen's favorite sexting app, Kik. Their server is located in Ontario, Canada making it more difficult for law enforcement to work their way through the Canadian legislation which is cumbersome and loses valuable time when searching for a missing child. This is especially dif-ficult if a predator is soliciting a teen, making sexual advances, or if a teen disappears when they sneak out to meet their new "friend." Law enforcement is greatly handicapped in gaining information on a predator who is using an app that transmits through a server in a foreign country. Most parents never consider this aspect when choosing appropriate apps for their child.

Author's note: As we are ready to go to print with this book, Kik management has announced a change in corporate direction. They are now saying they will be more responsive in assisting law enforcement in responding to subpoenas and even participating with National Center for Missing and Exploited Children and the Virtual Global Task Force in the scanning and reporting of Kik messages for inappropriate images including nudity. We applaud this effort.

All too often, a teen lives alone in a cyber world. There is no dialogue about right and wrong. In fact, there does not appear to be a right and wrong. There is no dialogue about the morality of killing. Killing is necessary to succeed. Evil is an obstacle to be overcome, without a true understanding of what evil is all about. Evil is not thought of in terms of spirituality and God being the *only* entity greater than evil. There is no exploration of real life experience with a prostitute. No fear of STDs. No allowance for a two-person interaction where the other person expresses feelings. No empathy for the devastation your actions may create. No personal responsibility for your decisions. In some games, there is a "spiritual" realm. The fight against evil. All sorts of personal and moral compromise are necessary to win. Many video games are designed to make evil appear appropriate.

In real life, one would think that a father might dialogue with a son about the issues surrounding hiring a prostitute. Doubtfully in real life would a father advise a son that it would be okay to kill her so you do not have to pay her. In real life, there are consequences for such actions, perhaps life in prison for murder. However, in the cyber world, there are no consequences, or even worse, the consequences are that you are awarded with "winning." The question is: at what point does the lack of dialogue about exploring the morality of your cyber decisions spill over into real life?

Or does it?

Here is the bottom line to Digital Morality. Apps, video chat rooms, live streaming, and online gaming all open up a whole new world for a young person. It is two-way dialogue that introduces your child to literally millions of ideas and concepts and *yes*, people. In my work in human trafficking, I see almost daily how this goes wrong. Parents hand the keys to the entire world with a lecture and often a threat, and then walk away and pray that it will all work out. That is ludicrous. It is not a secret world. In fact, just the opposite.

More people than you have met in your entire lifetime can now influence your child.

Some are good. Some are evil. Without dialogue, a child will believe the lie that what is done on the Internet is okay because it is not real. It is important for parents to have ongoing dialogue about building character on and off the Internet. It is important that they understand predators are seeking low-hanging fruit, and to teach them how to be strong and difficult to groom and recruit. It is important that parents help their teens understand that morality is important to character, whether it is in real life interaction or a virtual relationship.

CHAPTER FOUR

THE NUMBING DOWN OF AMERICA

Often I will hear my friends and colleagues talk about the "dumbing" down of America. The situations they are referring to have to do with the way people learn and the knowledge young people have today. An old timer will often talk about the fact that many young people who work in retail stores have trouble doing math or making change when handling the cash register. A lot of this has to do with the way our educational system has chosen to impart knowledge. As long as there are calculators and computers, a person does not need to add, subtract, multiply, or divide. However, take that same young person away from technology and they can barely function. In the same way that parents are uneducated about technology, a young person is dysfunctional without technology. We truly are living in the age of transition.

Much of the premise of Common Core Teaching Curriculum was conceived based on the idea that massive amounts of data are now at a person's fingertips, and therefore the belief that it is better to educate young people how to integrate the information into their day-to-day lives, rather than memorizing or learning basic facts and formulas such as math, algebra and geometry.

Personally, I am more concerned about the *numbing* down of America than the dumbing down of America. I think it is important to look at the underlying feelings related to Internet relationships and personal Internet usage. As we have previously discussed, children play violent animated video games but they *say* they don't feel a reaction to violence because it is all a game. It is what they have to do to win. I find it fascinating that most of these video games are created in a setting based on mystic, sorcery, wizardly, and sometimes occult settings. To be engaging, the graphics and sound are enhanced to create an addictive and satisfying interaction, adrenaline rushes are the primary desired effect. The player is fully engaged in the process of living in the fantasy world, and some of the newest games boast advanced technology called "first person experience." Certainly few would argue that the player does not experience any emotion at all. To the contrary, they are highly engaged, excited, and even committed to the mission of winning. People cannot do that unless they are feeling something.

Most researchers of video games will tell you that when players are having difficulty obtaining an acceptable number of points or is having trouble moving to the next level, they experience dejection and sadness. Obviously the players are experiencing normal emotions. Most players will tell you they are experiencing a phenomenon known as the "Tetris Effect." Dr Andrew Doan explores this in his book, *Hooked on Games*. The Tetris Effect is in essence a scenario where the player will continue playing the game mentally even when he is not accessing a computer. The Tetris Effect implies that the player is experiencing emotions about the game and specific scenarios, or he would not continue to work on the play in his head. The Tetris Effect is probably what is going on with your son when you take him to dinner and he answers in single syllables. So it is evident to me that game players are experiencing emotions while playing, and most of the emotions could be considered quite normal.

However, when you ask these same players how they feel when they kill another avatar, wipe out a virtual city, hire a prostitute and kill her to save their payment, these same players will tell you they do not experience guilt or shame because they are "just playing the game" and need to win. One of the troubling aspects of gaming is the need for you and your guild to win at all costs. The other troubling aspect is that in the virtual world, there are no real life consequences to their actions. Somewhere deep inside, I would hope our young people know that killing and prostitution do not truly represent winning. However, without dialogue, we give them no way to search their soul and verbalize that. In fact, killing as winning is reinforced over and over. They are being desensitized.

In my opinion, these players are being dishonest when denying their feelings, or we are creating a world full of young people who are able to enter a sociopathic state where they are not responsible for any of their decisions and actions. The primary emotion they appear to be driven by is fear of rejection. To be successful, an avatar must maintain a high level of points and be accepted by their guild and guild manager.

We are using gaming to teach decision processes in an environment where there are no real life consequences for actions. I believe that is significant.

We recently read of a case where a six-teen-year-old guy was playing World of Warcraft and he was not particularly adept. He was having trouble getting enough points so that major guilds would be interested in inviting him to join. He did get into a guild, but was in desperate need to get his point level up. In addition to earning the points through play, players could use credit cards to purchase equipment for their avatar with bitcoins. This young man could not get his hands on a credit card, so he asked his guild manager if he could borrow some bitcoins. The guild manager loaned him the bitcoins, but asked for his naked photo in exchange. The guild manager turned out to be a pervert who participated in one of the largest child porn rings in the world. He took the boy's naked photo and put it on the porn ring to literally thousands of perverts. Then he blackmailed the guy for more photos and wanted to meet up for sex.

Think about the feelings the young man experienced. Fear of being found out by friends and family. Feelings of shame and guilt for having been duped, and embarrassment and trauma as men wanted to engage in sex with him. He perceived himself as being heterosexual and normally would have not reached out to men.

Think about the nightmare his life had become. What if his folks or school friends found out? He felt dirty. He felt trapped. My guess is that the parents (assuming he was part of an intact family) would notice a change in his behavior but would not be informed enough to help dialogue through the situation. Most likely, without intervention the young man would retreat from social scenes and become depressed and withdrawn. Somewhere there was a parent saying, "I don't know what has happened, but he has changed somehow."

Interesting to me in these situations is that the young person does not appear to be able to project out how these scenarios could go wrong before they send the photo. There is a desperate need to inform and educate young people so they can learn from others' mistakes, and that is the work of Million Kids.

That is also the work of parenting. It is critical and urgent to share on a regular basis with teens stories of how other teens have been groomed and exploited. These stories appear daily on Million Kids' (Riverside) Facebook page, if you need examples. It is this type of scenario that offers the greatest opportunity for dialogue and exploration between parent and teen. Most teens are hormonal and have limited cognitive reasoning skills. Their ability to project out the potential results is restricted. If the parent and the teen have an open honest relationship and the parent has taken the time to sit with the teen and understand the dynamics of how the game or video chat rooms work, then there is a huge opportunity to take the secrecy out of Internet relationships and use all this as a learning tool for the young person. It is possible that if dialogue is developed in a supportive fashion, it will actually meld the bond between parent and teen as they explore the possibilities in a non-hostile setting.

There is an important element to make this work. *The parent must become educated on every website and every game a teen plays.* A parent or grandparent *does not need to know how to use every app or play every game*, but they should be able to sit with their child and say, "Show me your avatar." "What does his character stand for?" "What is his name?" "What do the tattoos on your character represent?" "How do you get points?" "Who is your guild manager?" "What do you know about him?" "Are there guild players you chat with?" "What do you know about them?" If your child wants to install a new app, then research it with them. Look at the pros and cons and discuss the good points as well as the dangers. Use this opportunity to help your child develop good decision making processes.

This may sound daunting, but if you start today and get involved one app, one game at a time, then your life and the life of your teen will be greatly enhanced. I suspect if it is done with the right tone and attitude of having them teach you, your overall relationship can go from distrust to humorous. It could actually be fun if you approach it right. After all, you *are* the parent. Enjoy learning new things, and show your child how much better your lives are when you actually engage with each other.

Equally important is the need for a parent to develop dialogue about the "feelings" being experienced in the game. "What do you think about the killing?" "They are asking you to do something unethical." "Would you think it is unethical in real life?" "Why is that okay in a game and not in real life?" "They are asking you to select a sex act with a prostitute." "How do you feel about that?" Without outside dialogue, a teen will never stop and sort through the ethics of life. Real or virtual, morals should be explored and understood.

I believe the denial of feelings and the unwillingness to label digital actions as moral or immoral are "numbing" down our youth. From the beginning of the introduction of the Internet, there has been a sense of omnipotence. Early on people shared their greatest fears, said things electronically they would normally never say publically, and have without forethought made announcements of their personal lives that they would never say in person. It is almost as if people think the Internet is equivalent to a priest in a confessional, and they spill their guts. Working with young people, I am always amazed at the number of young people willing to send their naked or masturbating photo across the World Wide Web. When sending the photo, they feel entitled and brazen, but then when the ensuing tsunami of bullying, criticism, teasing, taunting, and blackmail sets in, the victim feels damaged, shamed, and victimized. My experience in working with these teens is that the damage they experience from this exploitation is processed similarly to or the same as if they have been physically violated.

My point here is that up until now, parents and teens alike have bought into the myth that engaging in immoral behavior in a digital world is acceptable because there are no consequences to their actions. However, I would suggest there *are* consequences no one wants to look at. I believe this is true of teens that act out in video chat rooms. Yes, they are just being silly, but they are making a moral statement, creating a virtual resume of themselves. More important, they are creating a moral roadmap for their internal barometers. They have become desensitized, and each decision about what is ethical, appropriate, and morally acceptable will slowly deteriorate to a point where there is no forethought given to totally elicit behavior. I believe there is a trend of denying that a player is experiencing negative emotions so they can continue to fulfill their adrenaline addiction. It is "selective admission."

Let me share with you a new phenomena taking place on the Internet. The Internet is fast expanding in capacity and bandwidth, making it possible to have hundreds of thousands of people hooking up by video chat room. One of these apps is Omegle, where a person signs up for the service and then they randomly receive the next available person into their video chat room. They have no idea who they may be receiving. Their motto is "talk with strangers". These chat rooms are a venue for America's teenagers to meet up with new people and create entertainment that obviously challenges everyone's inhibitions. The more bizarre behavior in these videos, the better. Go ahead and look this up on YouTube. You will see America's teenagers when obviously mom and dad are not home. I am blown away at how young these kids are that are agreeing to allow total strangers into their lives through the Internet.

Recently I saw an Omegle/YouTube video where a guy was bathing in front of the whole world. To date, it has 3.8 million viewers. If you look at it, turn the sound off. This young man appears to believe his primary talent is limited to bathing in front of the whole world. He has nearly a single word vocabulary. Other than the obvious that this guy is one bucket short of a full load, he was sharing with the world that he had no self-respect. Look at the viewers he is entertaining. Some are very young. Some offer to have (a variation of) sex with him. What is worrisome is that this chat video is going out randomly to all available Omegle participants. There is a similar YouTube/Omegle video of a young man "taking a poop" that has 1.4 million viewers. Now that takes talent and intelligence!

There are many other Omegle/YouTube videos, such as the "hanging man prank", which also had 5.6 million viewers to date. In this Omegle video, a fourteen or fifteen year old male pretends to hang himself over and over. The fact that most people feel this was just a prank for attention and move on is simply a statement of how far Omegle is willing to go to make money by selling ads on sites like these. It also shows how little value our young people place on making certain they meet high quality individuals who will enhance their lives. In my personal opinion, every parent should recognize the Omegle logo and insist their teen never have it on their smartphone or computer. It is obvious that most of these young people who are making and receiving these videos have little or no parental supervision.

For hundreds of years, young people have had the choice of participating in high quality school activities or hanging out in sleazy places with low life friends. In real life, most parents would never allow a teen to take the low road, but somehow today because parents are naïve and uninformed, they will buy the devices for their teens and refuse to be responsible for the results.

I recommend that if you are buying a teen a smartphone, it would better for both of you to educate yourselves together and learn each website and app that you agree to access. Then learn to dialogue about the pros and cons of each, the assets and dangers, and allow the teen to experience an adult's insights to project out the consequences.

Perhaps I am going out on a limb and offending some, but truthfully, if a parent decides to purchase a smartphone for a teen without participating in the terms of usage and resulting behaviors, then they share the blame for the consequences. The purchase of a smartphone should be along the lines of driver's education. The teen needs to understand that while the smartphone can take them to many wonderful places and teach them amazing things, it can also result in being harmed, exploited, and in some cases the result has been suicide when used inappropriately.

The same is true of online gaming and MMORPGs (World of Warcraft, Black Ops, Minecraft, Grand Theft Auto to name a few). Parents give in to teens' nagging to get the latest gaming technology without ever joining in the gaming with the teen. Just as I am writing this, there is a news release about a fourteen-year-old girl who was playing Minecraft and met a twenty-five-year-old guy from Texas. They exchanged flirtations and over a period of two years the relationship became sexual in nature. The twenty-five-year-old male allegedly sent videos and photos of a sexual nature to the young teen. The teen was twelve when the relationship began. It sounds like "love" to me. He is twenty-five years old and she is twelve years old! At some point, the girl's mother became aware of the situation. I can only assume it was after she had been playing for a couple of years. The older male drove from Texas to Michigan to meet the girl. When the mother intervened, the male was found to be carrying a thirteen-inch knife. He was arrested.

Our first inclination is to believe that this story ended well since the police were summoned to apprehend the man and no one was actually physically hurt. Not so fast. Here is a twelve-year-old girl who has lost her innocence. Never again will she get a thrill out of holding a thirteen year old's hand or having a first love down the street. She has processed her twelve-year puberty through the lens of hard-core pornographic images with a twenty-five year old predator for over a year. I would predict that if they do not get this girl counseling and allow her to process her guilt and shame-based inclinations, she will be at a much higher risk for being recruited into sex trafficking than your average twelve year old. Research indicates that at least seventy percent of prostitutes were previously sexually molested and although this girl has not been physically touched (to our knowledge); she has in fact been emotionally and psychologically exploited. Time and time again as I talk with survivors of sex trafficking they tell me of stories where they were violated long before meeting their pimp or predator.

This same article cites a separate story of a forty-six-year-old man who was arrested in 2011 for beating up a thirteen-year-old boy because the teen killed him in the popular game, Call of Duty. I take this side trip to share these stories because I want parents, educators, and law enforcement to understand the trend that is taking place here. While some online gaming certainly has its good points, other games create an environment of secrecy punctuated with violence and sexuality. All too often, we are placing our children in a *virtual incubator.* This incubator masks the day-to-day interactions that allow total strangers to groom our young people, all in the guise of being part of a guild or just playing with teammates who can be any and every predator around the globe. Unless a parent is prepared to sit beside their teen or preteen and participate, it is the same as dressing them up and letting them troll on the sidewalk to see who they can attract. Where is the sanity in this?

CHAPTER FIVE

CROSSING A THRESHOLD
FIRST PERSON EXPERIENCE

For several generations now, teens have been raised on violence. Parents were concerned when television shows progressively engaged in more killing, explicit violence and some nudity. Then movies became much more realistic as technology increased and the public adjusted their standards as to what was acceptable in exposing young people to violence, killing, torture scenes, and explicit sexuality. Video games were introduced, and again parents and teens adjusted what was acceptable for exposure to young minds. Rap music appeared to break the mold as extremely graphic language and hip hop music told stories of killing and violence and "hos" (whores) and pimps. Again we adjusted. Movie stars and rock stars such as Madonna and Britney Spears appeared to cross the threshold of what was proper and appropriate for teens, followed by Lindsay Lohan and Rihanna.

Currently Miley Cyrus appears to be determined to sink to the bottom by flaunting immoral excesses.

For several years, there appears to be a race as to who can be the raunchiest advertiser, with Abercrombie and Fitch leading the way for bestiality and Carl's Jr. trying to convince young people that it is enticing to have ketchup run down your mostly naked breasts while slithering around, trying to get your mouth over a hamburger. What is important in these examples is that these advertisers are not necessarily selling their products, but rather lowering the threshold of dignity and values within our society.

Until recently, technology was "viewed" as an outside participant watching a story unfold. As previously mentioned, in 2015, both World of Warcraft and Grand Theft Auto V released games that boast new technology called "first person experience." This technology is only one example of how sophisticated and progressive technological capabilities are advancing in gaming. Several of these games have reported that more than one hundred million dollars was spent to develop the game and most game-producing companies expect to net out over one billion in sales. This is big business. Animation capabilities are simply mind-boggling. Sometimes it is easy to believe the characters were filmed live. The artistic endeavors being undertaken in the gaming world creates vivid story lines in extraordinarily real mystical settings. Demons and dragons come alive in ways we would never have thought possible, even five years ago.

Even before this latest technological advance, there was a significant difference between being a "viewer" and being a participant. I believe that it is critical for parents to understand the difference between watching a movie and being engaged as a player in a game. Parents may be cognitive of the difference but I am not certain that most parents have thought through the details related to how that may impact their child.

You may take your child to a movie and view violence and sex. Most likely you and your child will view it only one or two times. The violence and sex are happening to the characters on the screen. As a viewer, you process it and you may even recall a particular scene from time to time afterward. You and your child may discuss certain aspects of the movie. You return home and go on with your life.

The difference is that in gaming, the participant creates one or more "avatars" and his actions control the direction of the game. His character takes on the various quests, which determines his success in the game. His success or failure affects the success or failure of his guild. This means the emotions that are being processed are not focused on a movie character that terminates when the movie is over. This is a subtle but explosive difference. We have truly crossed a cataclysmic threshold and few people have taken notice.

A movie is experienced in a fixed time period with a plot that is happening "out there." While we may be able to empathize and continue to reflect on the story, when it is over, it is over. Gaming crosses an important threshold. Your success or failure in the game is based on how you perform as the avatar. You are in control. You are responsible. You decide and you either win or lose. Your guild manager and other guild players accept you or not.

While you are operating through your avatar (your alter ego), you process the emotions with the same real life emotions as if it is really happening. You kill the enemy and take out a city and you are *up*. You are a hero. You lose and you feel depressed and begin to strategize how to do it differently. You are *down*. The emotions in winning are real and the frustration and dejection from losing are real. However, we convince ourselves that the illicit, immoral behaviors we have exhibited in the game are okay because they are not real. It is again, selective morality.

As someone who works with parents of delinquent teens and at-risk children, I believe we are all kidding ourselves. Gaming manufacturers and video chat room distributors such as Omegle are perpetrating one of the biggest lies of all time on our society. Our children are groomed emotionally through what they experience on the Internet.

I contend that if a game is addictive (Clash of the Clans advertises it is the most addictive game ever) and if the player becomes elated or depressed based on winning or losing, then the player is emotionally engaged in the game. They want you to believe that the immorality they experience (killing, prostitute sex, mass murder, etc.) is okay because it is just a game and not real. I am saying we have crossed a threshold with technology. There is a *significant* difference.

Our society expects young people to navigate back and forth between real life reality where we expect decision making with standards and consequences and a fantasy world of gaming where there are few morals and no real live consequences for their actions. Except even in a fantasy world of gaming, if you make a real life decision to send your naked photo to your avatar buddy, then there CAN BE REAL LIFE CONSEQUENCES. How do we teach our young people discernment? This is true folly if we think this is OK. I have seen case after case where this goes horribly wrong. And that is one of the reasons I have written this book.

Earlier I introduced you to Dr. Doan is also a neuroscience researcher on addiction for the U.S. Navy and a friend of mine. Dr. Doan and his wife, Julie, often make presentations to universities and large audiences about the psychological and neurological impact gaming has on young people. They especially explore the chemical and emotional impact gaming has on the developing brain of a young person. Their presentation conveys many fascinating findings regarding cortisol and testosterone changes that have been discovered through researching individuals who have spent long hours playing various games. Their research concludes that there is a significant psychological and neurological impact, especially if you are dealing with an early pubescent teen that plays online games many hours a day. One cannot read Dr. Doan's research without walking away with the knowledge that as much as gamers and game manufacturers would have you believe otherwise, gamers *do* experience the emotional impact of their actions while gaming.

You can view Dr. Doan's work by going to www.real-battle.org.

This is an interesting phenomenon. Players say they experience no guilt when they kill, yet they blame themselves profusely when they lose a play and cost themselves and their guild success. They strategize, they fantasize, and they manipulate and maneuver to do it differently the next time. So the emotions they admit to are related, not to their own sense of morality (killing, having ordered a blow job from a prostitute), but rather whether they are winning or losing and being accepted by others. Is this about being desensitized or is this about having selective morality where the end justifies the means?

As I previously mentioned, "Clash of the Clans," (a MMORPG) advertises itself as, "The most addictive game ever." How can a game be the most addictive ever if the player is *not* feeling anything? Au contraire. I would argue that the player *does* feel. It is all about winning. Winning brings elation. Losing brings rejection and despondence. Ask any player, and they will tell you that they are addicted to the highs and lows of the game. The design of the games gives them a false sense of "control" of being able to guide their own digital destiny and earn the respect and approval of their guild and guild managers. The avatar (the player's alter ego) buys equipment and earns points and maneuvers through ever-increasing difficult challenges, living vicariously, fighting evil and winning at all costs. As you become more and more successful, you are deeply involved with your guild manager and responsible to your team for succeeding. The pressure builds. The guild manager will get you up at 3:00 A.M. so your team wins. The guild is counting on you to play *and to win*. Winning is the name of the game at all costs. It is not a coincidence that the women in the games wear tiny little outfits and have Barbie doll faces. Some flirt and engage with you. Some of the games even introduce elements of pornography. Combining sex and violence in a competitive setting controlled by an outside guild manager has proven to be an exploitative and addictive combination to teenage boys who are hormonal and seeking approval and success. I sometimes think of it as the "inevitable addiction."

There is another factor about gaming that needs to be professionally explored with scientific research. This issue has to do with the effect of sexual activity and pornography integrated within a video game that contains violence and conquering the enemy. I remember reading an autobiography by Ted Bundy, one of the major serial killers of our time. He said that he could actually remember the day that he married violence and sex and the intense emotional impact that he experienced. Remember, in many games, this same violence and sexual activity is experienced in "first person." Prior to gaming, most people would never encounter a scenario where they were introduced to sexual experiences while combating demons with violent scenes of high-powered guns and explosives.

Many games are set in scenes or themes related to the occult, magic, sorcery, wizardry, and mystical environments. Now we consider it "entertainment" for our children. In fact, in real life, a sexual experience involves give and take, listening and engaging, pleasing and being pleased, taking into account the emotional responses of your mate. In gaming, sex is a one-dimensional experience and often is more about reinforcing one's own ego. As in all gaming, it is paramount that the level of violence and sex escalates to keep the players engaged. It is inevitable that young people who are routinely exposed to sexual images and audio will become addicted and will need ever increasing tantalization to be satisfied.

David Stewart is a licensed marriage and family therapist in Riverside, California, who specializes in working with men and couples who are addicted to sex or pornography. David and I have had discussions about the impact pornography has on a young mind, and how quickly the mind is groomed to accept accelerating levels of depravity. David has shared that most men remember the first time they saw pornography as a child and that experience molded their future addiction, especially if it was hard-core porn. Today, pornographic images are so intertwined in our advertising, music, television, social media and games that victims may not be able to pinpoint the exact event. However, youth ministers tell me that they are seeing a true epidemic of twelve, thirteen and fourteen-year-old boys addicted to porn. We hear of regular cases where girls are becoming addicted to pornography.

I would submit that most teens do not realize how deeply addicted they are to pornographic images until they find themselves acting out in an inappropriate manner that is suddenly unacceptable to society. They may even be surprised at their own behavior. This can be confusing for young people, and they won't know where to go for help. If these young people do not get professional assistance for their addiction, they will be driven by dark urges and will find themselves acting out in ways that will destroy their future careers and family life. Our society has a tendency to treat pornography as just another type of art, and like all things there are varying levels of impact and intensity. However, I would submit to you that a thirteen-year-old hormonal boy with an undeveloped brain will be greatly corrupted if he consistently lives in a world of violence and sex, and to get the approval of others, he must win. This is a lethal combination and our society will pay the price.

Certainly, there needs to be more research into what is driving the lack of inhibitions many young people are displaying on the Internet. As we have explored in the previous chapter, Omegle, YouTube, and a myriad of other websites and apps have literally thousands of videos and photos that indicate a complete lack of inhibitions on the part of the participant. Many teenage boys are easily lured into forwarding a photo with a full array of their nakedness with the slightest inclination that a girl will be impressed. The same goes for many young girls sending topless photos and more on request of someone they have never met. I know because when this goes horribly wrong, these young people call me to see if I can help them get their photos back. I cannot.

As we examine the various YouTube videos of chat room encounters of teenagers partially naked, emulating sex scenes, pretending to hang themselves, appearing to be the devil, displaying toilet functions, etc., one cannot help but wonder what kind of morality base the kids in these videos are operating from. Are they proud of themselves? Do they feel they have accomplished something to boast about? Do they believe this is their only asset so flaunt it?

Do they feel guilt or shame? Or perhaps their self-esteem is so low they figure they have nothing to lose? It appears there is little forethought going into the consequences of posting these photos until they are being used to groom a victim for sex trafficking or exploitation and then there is panic on how to get the photos back.

As I write this, I am cognizant that all of us are grappling with the changes in our society that affect parenting and our young people because of the extreme technological advancement taking place around us. Video chat rooms are a relative new technology that has enabled websites like Omegle and ooVoo and others to engage our children in ways never before possible. As I look at how realistic animation now appears in many advertisements and websites and games, I am struck by how quickly technology is changing our exposure to surreal situations that could not be accomplished in depicting real life. The result is a world of Dungeons and Dragons, and World of Warcraft and four Chan, a despicable site that promotes anonymous posts and hoaxes.

My point is that we are just getting started. The technological changes that have impacted our society are in their infancy.

As this book is in its second printing we are being introduced to LIVE STREAMING. The most famous are Periscope and Meerkat. This technology is basically Facebook on steroids. A child can make a live cam of their activity (or your home) using their video and sound on their smart phone and broadcast it around the world to literally millions of people. Some teens already have tens of thousands of followers. People all over the world can circle in to your community and hook up with a broadcaster and use the GPS tracking to pinpoint the location. As we recently explored this capability we found a 14 year girl giving a tour of her parent's home while they were away. But let's say your 14 year old wants to show off her new bellybutton ring. Tens of thousands of folks can follow her and I am sure that ALL OF THEM are lovely Christian people, Seriously? This is a magnet for predators, pimps and pedophiles and we must STOP AND TAKE NOTE and explore the good and the bad of this technology with our young people.

Where we are today with technology will appear amateurish and simplistic in another five years. It is imperative that we stop and access the impact on our children's moral compass. If we do not, it is my experience in working with exploitation and sex trafficking that thousands of strangers from around the global will do it for us. It is time to take a hard look at reality and take appropriate actions to put the power back into parenting. Just because our behavior is displayed globally on the Internet does not exempt us from being (and raising) morally responsible adults. Technology is a powerful tool if used appropriately but it can equally be an exploitative tool if we remain naïve and allow our children to lead the way by living in a secret cyber world.

CHAPTER SIX

TRUTH IN A DIGITAL WORLD

In decades past, *truth* was an unstated expectation. It was part of morality. To be a person of character required honesty. A man was expected to be a man of his word. If it was in print, you could believe it to be true. Many journalists lost their reputations and even their jobs for printing some statement or fact that was not true, or could not be proven to be true, or even had shades of a "little white lie." In the Bible, the ninth commandment is, "Thou shall not lie." However, somewhere along the way, we began to descend a slippery slope.

Maybe it started with President Richard Nixon and Watergate, when he was convicted of lying to a grand jury. As a Baby Boomer, I have a tendency to think it began when President Bill Clinton, theoretically the most powerful man in the free world, faced the entire world on television, wagging his finger and saying, "I did not have sexual relations with *that* woman." I remember the resulting radio talk shows and television commentaries when it became obvious he had point-blank told a bold-faced lie to the entire world. There was a common theme. "Lying is okay if it is about sex." "Everyone lies about sex." "What did you expect the man to do? He was caught. He was just trying to protect his wife." On and on.

When you think about it, our society accepts untruths every day. "Your call is important to us," while making customers hold on the phone nearly forty-five minutes. Or try this one: "You get the second one absolutely free, if you call now. Just pay a *small* shipping and handling fee." The cosmetic industry thrives on promising you will look ten years younger in only two weeks.

President George W. Bush led us into war based on the belief of "weapons of mass destruction" in Iraq. He may have believed that to be true, but history so far has not proven that out. Regardless of the intent, today we are all a little less certain of real truth. Even our current President looked the public in the eye and stated, "If you like your plan, you can keep your plan" (Obamacare). Whether that was a deliberate untruth or simply a good promise gone bad, it leaves society sorting through whether there is still truth to the idea that a man is only as good as his word. This generation, alas, nearly the entire universe has come to regard a concept that says if it is about politics, *truth* is optional. The message being played out to the public is that if the end justifies the means, then it is okay. "Winning at all costs" is the message being sent, and you must play to win regardless. Truth in a digital world appears to have lost its moral value.

Let's take a look at how that translates to today's young people as they live and breathe on the World Wide Web. The beauty of the Internet is that it is like the Wild West, with almost no restrictions. Individuals posting on the Internet can be honest or crooked. They can make fantastic claims with no need to back them up. No one person (or corporation) is punished for publishing dishonest claims. Buyers beware, and purchase at your own risk. You have won the lottery and only need to advance $1,000 to collect, and your uncle in Nigeria is wiring you money. Even Wikipedia warns in their various postings that although an alleged "fact" is posted on their site, it may not be true as they receive information from millions of contributors that they are unable to verify as to the accuracy of the post.

If discerning the truth is difficult in real life, face-to-face situations for adults, how do you teach discerning truth to children in a digital world where truth has little verification?

On the Internet, you can pretend to be anyone you want to be. Most young people are familiar with the term "catfishing," which describes a person pretending to be someone when you are really someone else. Most young people have been raised using the Internet and most are familiar with the idea that there are many fraudulent claims and many people claiming to be someone they are not.

However, when talking with teens, I am always amazed at their naivety. As I have previously mentioned, teenagers appear to be incapable of projecting out the dangers they are in, or the level of exploitation they may endure by meeting up with a so-called friend who is really a predator. If they are on a dating site, then they are cautious. Oftentimes in social media or online gaming, they meet an attractive guy or girl and they are easily duped. In my experience, the minute the teen starts to think in terms of a relationship, they drop all desire to verify the validity of the new acquaintance's claims unless there are significant warning signs. It is as if most teens still utilize the "real person" experience because they *want* everything they are experiencing in real life to be true on the Internet.

The Internet provides teen with complex challenges that few are mature enough to navigate without compromise. On the one hand, they relish having total secrecy regarding their interactions with others, and they assume they will be wise enough to stay safe. On the other hand, few young people can resist the thrill, the sexiness of meeting a gorgeous hunk or fabulous blonde who can make them think they have found their one true love. The insidious nature of an Internet relationship is that a predator can pretend to be what the teen is waiting to find with all their heart. All it takes is a small amount of information and the teen begins to fall in love with their own fantasy. We will explore this more in the chapter on Fantasy Relationships.

Discerning truth could be the greatest challenge to *all* people in the twenty-first century. Never before in history has so much information been presented to an individual in one day. How do we teach our children to discern the truth? Even more interesting: How does a parent guide a child in selecting appropriate materials in forming critical thinking patterns, developing character, defining appropriate moral behavior and forming healthy attitudes about sexuality and respect in relationships? As previously mentioned, this becomes even more challenging because more than seventy percent of teens believe that what they do on the Internet should be secret.

Here are some amazing statistics from www.youtube.com:

- More than one billion unique users visit YouTube each month
- Over six billion hours of video are watched each month on YouTube—that's almost an
- hour for every person on Earth
- One hundred hours of video are uploaded to YouTube every minute
- Eighty percent of YouTube traffic comes from outside the U.S.
- YouTube is localized in sixty-one countries and across sixty-one languages
- According to Nielsen, YouTube reaches more U.S. adults ages eighteen through thirty-four than any cable network

What is important in understanding the mind-boggling statistics regarding YouTube is the realization that while they claim that one hundred hours of video are uploaded every minute, there is no analysis, no verification of truth process. Anybody can make a video about anything and make audacious and outlandish claims with no accountability or repercussions. In fact, often it is the most outlandish and ridiculous video that gets millions of hits from viewers.

There are other sites that are equally enticing to young people such as 321 Chat, Chatroulette, SpeedDate, and TinyChat. As technology expands capacity and speed, we are being introduced to a wide range of video chat rooms that encourage hooking up or coming together with total strangers. Viewers who participate in these chat rooms and interact with others on these sites have little means to authenticate their identity. This opens the door to an unending amount of perverts and seducers that a child would seldom encounter in real life, and even if they did they would not be tempted to engage in dialogue. The Internet is often the great equalizer, making even the most questionable individuals appear attractive. Verification of truth about a person you have not met before is extremely difficult for adults and even more challenging for a young person with little life experience and undeveloped cognitive and decision making skills. Yet, without a full understanding of the possible outcomes, parents all over the world hand their ten year old a device that opens the door to the entire world and hope and pray that it will all work out all right.

Now let's compare these websites with a more popular and sophisticated website like MeetMe.com. MeetMe.com was originally created to act as a kind of yearbook for teens, but after being acquired by a Latino social networking site Quepasa, it launched Charm, a mobile dating app. According to Wikipedia, MeetMe.com includes a virtual economy through which members earn money through games and spend "lunch money", the virtual currency. At its height of popularity, MeetMe.com was registering 86,000 new users per day and it is estimated that there 4.5 million users worldwide. MeetMe.com is similar to sites like Tagged that is based on finding new friends in your area using a GPS system. Theoretically, you need to be over eighteen years old to use MeetMe.com.

Here is the challenge. In the virtual world it is nearly impossible to monitor who really is of legal age, who is a sex offender, and who may be joining for the sole purpose of satisfying the perverted urges of a predator. There have been many cases of teens hooking up with predators on sites like MeetMe.com, Skype, Facebook, Kik and others and all too often the teen ends up being exploited or sex trafficked. In fact, nearly seventy percent of the cases of prostitution in Southern California involved recruitment through the Internet.

The great enigma of the twenty-first century is how to parent a young person in such a way that they can live in a world where perverts and predators can use social media as a grooming and recruitment tool without falling prey and becoming a victim. I believe it starts with both parent and teen being educated. It will take teamwork like never before in history, as both parties take the secrecy out of the Internet and explore the highs and lows of technology. It must start with a dialogue.

The challenge is that we are using games and electronics to teach even babies how to engage with others, how to learn, how to communicate, and that is good. The key is restricting communication to outsiders until they have reached an age where they can comprehend the dangers and learn safe ways to utilize technology without putting themselves in a position of vulnerability.

How do we teach them when to trust others and when to not? How do we teach a young person to discern what is true and what is accurate and what is real? How do we teach a child to ferret out when others are genuine in their electronic communications? How do they know if their "friend" is real when they want with all their heart to believe this friend thinks they are the most wonderful person on earth.

There is an added layer to this challenge. As I have previously mentioned, research statistics tell us that at least seventy percent of teens believe they have a right to secrecy. Most adults are technologically impotent. They are totally unaware, and most live such busy lives earning a living and meeting the challenges of daily lives. Many are techno-phobic and believe they are incapable of learning all about the Internet. That begs the question: How can a parent guide a child if they are ignorant about the child's world? Either they limit their child's access to the Internet, or they find a way to get informed so they can have a dialogue and explore the highs and lows with their child.

In my experience working with both teens and parents, there is a significant difference in a teen's risk-taking attitudes and willingness to put themselves out there, based on the types of parenting constraints they have been raised with. Those who have been raised in a strong parental household, who have regular dialogue about appropriate behavior, are going to be much less vulnerable to being groomed and recruited. Those parents who started early on laying out the example of what was moral and acceptable will not stop because new technology is changing their lives. A smart parent will do whatever it takes to equip themselves with the knowledge to have informed and exploratory dialogue.

One observation is that the parenting dilemma takes on a different dimension as the teen starts through puberty. Certainly this has always been true with all generations. The very nature of pubescent development is meant to teach independence, practice responsible decision-making, and learn accountability for your behavior. This has not and should not change because we now have the World Wide Web and MMORPGs. What has changed is the vast number, literally millions, of predators and strangers looking to access and influence your child. Also what has changed is the ease and speed with which your child can be accessed and influenced because of the web.

It would appear that in the cases I have worked with or been exposed to, there are usually three divergent paths that take place at puberty.

1.) The parent(s) has been actively involved in the child's life and they have strong dialogue between them. The parent realizes they need to become techno-savvy so they can continue to mentor their teen. They have a good balance of discipline, guidance, mentoring, and dialogue about the pros and cons of technological advances, and they have discussions about having a dignified and professional appearing social media persona and resume. The parent sets smartphone, app, social media, and gaming restrictions with reasonable limits, and at all times makes it clear to the young person that they can and will be checking their phone. Additionally, they make it clear that a violation of trust will result in the removal of the phone.

2.) A second scenario that I often encounter is that the parent(s) has been a good parent, but as the teen enters puberty the challenges escalate based on the changes within the relationship. Often the dynamics of the entire family and extenuating circumstances have created significant unresolved resentment and baggage in the parent-child relationship. Add rebellion, resentment, hostility and ever-changing hormone levels, and the communication becomes incremental and is often punctuated with distrust and accusations. The teen is alternating between wanting independence and still wanting others to be responsible for them. These are the first teens to declare their independence as a form of manipulation and demanding their right to privacy.

My experience is that this becomes exponentially significant if the teen is in a single-parent household, a broken home, or a home where there is a stepparent. It is my observation that the teen perceives their Internet world as their inherent right, their escape from reality. Often it is these teens who post a derogatory comment, send a naked photo, participate in sextortion with a photo they have received, or make themselves available to a suitor or new "friend."

A parent who is functioning in a parent-teen relationship with this level of conflict must seek outside counseling and work through these issues. I would recommend separate professional counseling for the teen. It is important that parents become informed *about* the Internet. They do not have to be able to use the Internet, but they need to be able to dialogue about it, recognize dangerous websites, apps, and games and understand why they are dangerous. We hope that this book will assist with that effort. It is the dialogue that is important. Without understanding the dangers and opportunities of each site, the teen, rather than the parent, holds all the power.

3.) The third scenario is the most concerning. It is impossible to define who is most at risk in this group, but certainly every young person who is living in vulnerable or exposed conditions is greatly at risk. These include foster children, independent living children, homeless children, runaway children, pregnant teens, and all teens left unsupervised for a significant amount of time. It includes children in households where the parent is physically, psychologically, and/or morally absent. I have seen wealthy, successful families that fit this category. A divorce results in perfectly fine teens being left alone for hours as the parents fight over who *has* to take the children this week. These people buy their children expensive video games and think nothing of the fact they are being exposed to pornography. I know really fine Christian people who are simply so busy with their own lives that they soothe their consciences by saying, "Everyone is doing it." It is my observation that even the best teen can be accessed, groomed, and exploited if they are consistently allowed to play on the Internet for several hours a day. These are the same wonderful parents who would never sit their child down in front of 1,000 perverts, and say to themselves he/she will be okay because he/she is a smart child. Really? These are thirteen-year-olds whose frontal lobes are not fully developed, are not capable of realistic cognitive reasoning, and by their very pubescence are seeking adventure, the opposite sex, and excitement. They are insecure and need to be loved and admired. That makes them vulnerable. So why on earth would we open the door to nearly a million predators and think that our child is so special they will defy all the odds?

The thoughts I am sharing are based on my observations of many parent and teen relationships that have struggled. Some have overcome and the teen has gone on to be a responsible adult who would make any parent proud. Some have lost their child to prostitution, as they could not turn the relationship around or they were uninformed and did not understand the dynamics of the situation until the child had been lured into exploitation. It is for those parents I have written this book.

A comment I often get from parents is, "My kid gets mad when I check their phone and it makes me feel bad when they get mad at me. Is it okay to check my teen's cell phone?" The answer from me is always an emphatic, "Absolutely." Not only can you check your teen's phone, you will be remiss as a parent if you do not. In most cases you are paying for the phone and it is a privilege no different than driving a car or extending a curfew. I believe a good analogy is: if you saw your child standing on a railroad track and there was a speeding train coming down the tracks, you would do everything within your capability to drag the child out of the way. If in doubt, just think of your teen's phone as a speeding train. You (or your teen) will not get hurt if you are not standing on the tracks.

One of my favorite lines of all time is from a top government official from El Salvador. He said,

"Only in America is a child's bedroom considered a separate nation."

How true. Children have a way of making a parent wallow in guilt for caring enough to protect them. I think the best response to give to a child who demands privacy with their smartphone is that they should not be doing anything they would not want to show to their mother, their father, their future employer, future spouse, their teacher, and their pastor. They need to understand as much as they believe what they do on the web is private, nothing could be further from the truth. What they put on the web is probably the *least* private thing they ever do.

Let me give you an example. I know of a teenage girl who was in love with her teen boyfriend. He wanted a naked photo. She wanted him to love her, and she agreed. Then they got in a fight. The boyfriend thoughtlessly shared her photo with friends to get even and soothe his anger over the breakup. In less than twenty-four hours, this girl began to get offers for sex from New York and the U.K. So how private is that?

I find it an interesting dichotomy that teens consider what they do on the Internet to be a secret, and yet they willingly share their most private thoughts (and photos) on an electronic device that has the capacity to send it to millions of people around the world. Yet they believe their parents do not have a right to know. A smart parent will dialogue with their teen so there is a solid understanding that even if the parent does not know (yet), that does not mean it is a secret. It really comes down to the fact that if a teen is doing something they are not proud of, something they need to hide, then perhaps they should not post it on the Internet.

CHAPTER SEVEN

FANTASY RELATIONSHIPS

Now that we have explored the concept that discerning truth is one of the great challenges of this generation, it is important to understand how that might play out in Internet relationships. This exploration is as much about how a relationship is perceived and processed by an individual as it is about how predators might present themselves to a potential victim.

A couple of days after I presented at a large organization in the Los Angeles area, I was contacted by one of the leaders of the group. She shared with me a story that I believe is important for all parents and teens to understand. This was a single-parent household and both mother and daughter were exceptionally smart individuals and they enjoyed a strong relationship between them. The daughter was about to graduate from high school, had a 4.0 grade point average, and was anticipating continuing on to college. She also had a job and was responsible. Mom told me that she knew her daughter played games on X-Box, but she was not concerned as the daughter was mature, disciplined, and responsible.

After I spoke at the event, mom told me that she started to have some uncomfortable thoughts that perhaps she had been overlooking some warning signs in the relationship. The daughter was just six weeks from graduating high school and there had been what mom thought was just the normal year-end agitation. She decided she wanted to share with her daughter about my presentation on sex trafficking that she had recently heard. Mom told me that when she sat with her daughter and shared, the girl began to cry and she went to her bedroom and came back with a passport and an airline ticket to Ireland.

As mom relayed the story to me, I could easily see how this perfectly intelligent, beautiful young lady had been groomed without either mom or the daughter realizing it. Apparently the girl had been playing a game on X-Box with a guy who said he was twenty-eight and was from Ireland. Obviously, no one could really know. He could have been fifty-nine and from Rwanda or UAE. Over the nine-month period of playing on X-Box, this person had convinced the young lady to 1.) Quit her job, and 2.) Quit high school six weeks from graduating with a 4.0 average. Without mom's knowledge, she was able to secure a passport and accumulated the money to purchase an airline ticket to Ireland. The conversation with mom took place on Friday evening and the airline ticket was for Sunday morning. She later said that she did not plan to tell mom until after she arrived there because she did not want mom to stop her.

Often when I am presenting to high school students, we discuss this particular case. What is wrong with this scenario? Well, first, *anything* that has to be done in secret probably should not be done. I share with students that if you cannot be proud of who you are and what you are doing and whom you are doing it with, *you probably should not be doing it*. Secondly, it is obvious the man had no respect for her dreams. For this girl to quit school six weeks from graduating so she could not go on to college meant that he was asking her to give up her dreams for a prosperous future. There is also the obvious issue of how we could locate the girl if she got on a plane without anyone knowing where she was going. How do we find her? She could have easily been transported on to any part of the world and disappear without a trace. Fortunately, mom was an engaged and astute parent and the teen was exceptionally mature. Therefore an open dialogue ensued and a catastrophe was diverted. Often in my line of work that is not the case.

There is an important lesson here. This perfectly smart girl had been groomed. It is called a "fantasy relationship." On the Internet, this man could pretend to be anyone he thought she would fall in love with. Predators historically will look for a potential victim's secrets and dreams, and areas where he feels that they can bond. In subsequent conversations, they groom the victim by offering tidbits and morsels that are enticing and soothe the ego. They will address any known fears by reassuring the victim how mature and adept they are. They will fill in the blanks of their needs. "I am sorry you don't have a dad in your life. He doesn't know what he is missing by not knowing you. I will take care of you." "Hey, I think freckles are cute, they make you look young and happy." "I can understand why you don't like your mom's boyfriend. He looks like a real creep. I need to help you get away from there." "Hey, I get it that you hate school. So did I. Let's start a business together. You don't need a degree to make money. I already run my own business and make lots of money, so I can take care of you. School really is a drag." These are just a few examples of a vast array of tactics used in grooming.

If we examine real life relationships, we often take for granted the evaluation process that we utilize when we meet new people. Perhaps unconsciously we have a tendency to size up others. Instinctively, we evaluate by smell to determine if the person has good hygiene, which we subconsciously equate to self-respect and attention to detail. If they are well groomed and well dressed, we conclude that they have strong self-esteem and personal pride and are probably successful. We begin to make assessments. Do they have tattoos? Do they smoke? Do they brush their teeth? Do they have children? Are they wearing an ankle bracelet (on parole)? Are they married? How old are they? Do they have employment? Etc., etc. When we are in the physical presence of others, we observe and make judgments of others and we ask a lot of questions to show interest. It is the polite thing to do. Most important, it allows us the opportunity to take an objective look at others and determine if they are safe and attractive to us. Certainly even in person, predators can deceive others by pretending to be different than what they are, but it is easier and more likely we will recognize a potential predator in person than if they are pretending to be someone else on the Internet.

When predators are grooming and attempting to recruit victims on the Internet, a common tactic is to provide the target with just enough information to be enticing, and let the young person fill in the blanks with their own fantasy. In fact, the key element in grooming is to help the target create the fantasy.

It is a subtle but absolutely critical point.

Grooming is all about having the victim create their own fantasy. Then they own it!

In a nine-month relationship (based on our example above), two people who talk regularly would know a lot about each other. We would know if they are really twenty-eight or fifty-nine. We would know where they are physically located. We know if they regularly told the truth or sometimes lied. We would probably know their local reputation and if they were a well-known criminal or a leader in their church. We would begin to understand if they had been married multiple times and they were paying a lot of child support. We would know if they drove a nice car or were living on the street. We could observe if they were in multiple relationships with many women (or men). We would probably know if they were paying a huge amount of alimony or if they moved regularly because they could not pay the rent. We could make judgments about their attitude. Do they treat people with respect? Do they have an anger management issue? Are they generous or real cheapskates? Are they jealous and possessive of others? Do they value spirituality? Do they value truth? Are they controlling and dominating? Do they listen and are they empathetic? Are they depressed? Do they have healthy attitudes about sex or do they gravitate toward sleaze and pornography? Are they narcissistic or value others equally to themselves? My point here is that in a nine-month real relationship, we would know much about each other.

In working with families of sex trafficking victims, I think the concept of understanding the fantasy relationship may be one of the most critical issues of the entire recruitment and grooming process. In most recruitment cases, the pimp or predator just opened the door and painted a background of possibilities, but it was the victim who unwittingly filled in the blanks. That is the insidious nature of grooming, because when it is your own fantasy, you own it. You are obsessed with making your fantasy become your reality. I believe it is this obsession that makes working with young people so difficult. Certainly some of it is about trusting others, especially if they have come from the foster care system or a broken home or have been previously sexually violated. However, I believe the real challenge is breaking through the fantasy a victim has created and is holding onto with all their heart. They will defend their dream with all their might because they have no reality to return to.

The predator says, "You have cute freckles," and she hears, "He likes me so I must be valuable." The predator sees an Instagram and says, "You really look sexy in that photo," and she hears, "See, men really are attracted to me, so I am not so ugly after all." The predator says, "I am sorry you have not seen your dad for a while. He doesn't know what he is missing," and she hears, "Here is a sensitive man who will take care of me. I'll show my dad I am valuable to men." The predator says, "Come stay with me and we can make money together," and she hears, "He thinks I am smart and we will be successful together and I will show my mom I am not so stupid after all." All the while the predator is using tidbits and comments, the victim is building a fantasy of driving nice cars, being beautiful and loved and living in a nice place, and she is the center of her universe. Real success, like going to college or having a good job appears unobtainable to her because it looks hard and far away. She decides to take a shortcut.

It looks like the quick, easy, and fun way out of her current life. So she will defend that with all her heart.

In the situation I described above, mom asked me what should she do to stop her daughter from going to Ireland. I thought for a while and said, "Let's try this. Why don't you (mom) put on your best movie star hat and say to your daughter, 'Hey, if you love him, then I am going to love him too. If you think he is terrific our whole family is going to think he is great. So let's do this. Let's cash in your airline ticket and we will use that money to buy him an airline ticket to come over here and meet the whole family. That way he can be part of our family and we will learn to love him and you can finish school. Now, tell us everything you know about him.'"

There are several factors to consider in using that strategy. First, you are embracing and acknowledging her fantasy. If mom had said, "Over my dead body, you are not getting on an airplane and going to Ireland," the girl would have rebelled. Maybe she would have complied or maybe she would have snuck out, but she would have been hostile. She would have been defensive. She would have shut down emotionally and blocked the trust between them.

This girl desperately needed a mother who could acknowledge her dreams and embrace the fact that she has a right to dream. Truthfully, she needed a mentor to help her begin to dismantle the fantasy and embrace the accompanying loss that is sure to ensue. By saying to the girl, "If you love him, then we are going to love him," the mother can make a statement that she still believes in the girl even if she is not showing good judgment. Certainly she made a poor decision, but she valued the relationship with her mother enough to tell her the truth *before* she got on the plane and left. That is an excellent starting point for mom to reassure the girl that mom believes in her.

The greatest gift you can give another human being, especially a teenager, is to reassure them you believe in them.

By accepting her as a person even while not embracing her judgment, the mother has kept open the door of communication and given the girl an opportunity to explore other ways of evaluating the treasured relationship. Critical to this conversation is to invite the girl to share everything she knows about him. If this girl carries a 4.0 average, she is exceptionally intelligent. She will fairly quickly discern that she probably only knows five or six real facts about him. I would encourage this mother, and all parents who may find themselves in this situation, to begin to have their targeted child write down what they know. I have actually thought of creating a relationship evaluator exercise for parents to work with. If the mother were smart, she would make it into a game. "If this guy might be my son-in-law someday, then I want to get to know him."

What is his full name?

How old is he?

How tall is he?

How much does he weigh?

How did you meet him?

How long have you been talking with him?

What apps and social media is he on so you can help me get to know him? (And then look at each together, to help you build his profile)

What have we learned about him from his various profiles? (If a parent doesn't know how to do this, then this dialogue is a great way to learn)

Let's see how many photos we can find of him on the Internet. Is he alone or with friends?

What can we learn about him from his friends' comments on Facebook, Instagram etc.?

Has he ever appeared in a YouTube? Which ones? Can we look at them?

Has he ever been married? How many times?

Is he divorced? How do we know if the divorce is legal?

Does he have children or stepchildren? How many?

Did he finish high school and where?

Did he go to college and where?

Does he have a degree, and what kind?

Where does he work and for how long? If not long, then where did he work before?

What kind of dreams and aspirations does he have for a career?

Do you have any friends who have met him in person?

Do your friends talk with him on the Internet also? How do they know him? What do your friends think of him?

Has he ever become angry or mad at you or others?

Has he ever become threatening or abusive to you or others?

Has he ever asked you for a suggestive photo? (Don't ask if she sent it yet, this is helping her get a big picture of *him*)

Does he know you are about to graduate from high school? Is he excited about that for you?

Does he think you should go on to college?

Does he know about your dream to become a _____, and does he support that?

If you continue in this relationship, will you still be able to become a _____?

How does he feel about religion?

Does he think spirituality is important?

What is his favorite movie?

What is his favorite book?

What is his favorite song and favorite artist?

If he is outside the U.S., then find out if he has ever been to the U.S., where, and when.

Does he own a car? What kind of car? How old? Can he send you a photo of it?

Does he like to dance?

Does he go to the gym and work out?

Has he ever sent you a sexy photo of himself, and would you share it?

Has he ever suggested that you be in "business" together?

Has he ever said he would like to have sex with you?

Why is meeting him on this particular date so important to you? Why is this date so critical?

Since you met him playing a game on X-Box, can you show your mom your avatar? What is the avatar's name? What does your character stand for?

What do you know about the rest of the players in your guild?

Is he the guild manager?

What is his avatar's name and what does his avatar do in the game? Can we learn about him with his chat?

Would you be willing to share his chat with your mom? (Probably not, but worth a try.)

Here is my point with this exercise: If the girl met this guy in real life and they had a nine-month relationship, she would most likely know the answers to most of these questions. The idea of this exercise is not to trap the girl, not to make judgments on the girl, not to reprimand, discipline or accuse the girl. This exercise is meant as a dialogue to build trust between mother and teen and help the girl to understand that she really does not know much about him. It is meant to get her thinking. Part of the exercise is to help her get the sense of urgency out of the situation. If this relationship is meant to be a lifetime relationship (worth dropping out of school and flying secretly halfway around the world for), then why is there a sense of urgency? Would it not be better to take some time and ask a lot of these questions? Why does she need to drop out of high school six weeks from graduating and give up her dreams to meet him on this particular date?

I share this exercise with you to stimulate your thinking of how to run intervention if you know of a young person at risk. It certainly is not the end-all and be-all for every situation, but is meant to help readers understand the dynamics of a fantasy relationship. Obviously both mother and daughter were mature, intelligent individuals who already had a strong bond. It also shares with you just how vulnerable every teen is even in the most ideal home environment.

It is cases like these that have driven me to write this book. A stranger can mesmerize even the most astute teen and adult if they do not understand the grooming process. I am always amazed at the occasional attractive, smart housewife (or husband) who falls in love with an "Internet lover" even though they have a spouse and children at home. They become obsessed. They think about leaving it all behind because their online lovers are everything their husbands (or wives) are not. They do not realize they have created their own fantasy and have fallen in love with a fictitious character that probably has a lot more flaws and dangers than the situation they are living in.

Digital fantasy could well be the most corruptive societal force of this decade.

The case I shared with you above involved solid individuals who were spiritually grounded and had a strong bond. So anyone can be seduced.

What about those children who aren't so lucky? The vulnerability to a predator for a child in a compromised situation is exponential. The situations are always complex but almost always have the same dynamic. One or more of the parents have other priorities. By the time a child is twelve or thirteen, everyone is carrying a lot of baggage in the relationship. Many parents convince themselves that they have done their parental responsibility, and for the most part they fantasize that the child is nearly raised and the parent should be free to attend to many of the aspirations they have set aside for the last ten or twelve years. It is the parent's turn! *This could be the biggest fantasy of all.*

Newsflash, mom and dad, a twelve-year-old—even a thirteen-year-old—is *not* an adult. Their brain is just starting to mature. They have not developed consistent decision-making skills. They are fluctuating hormonally. They strive for independence and privacy, but desperately need *your* approval. Perhaps more so than any other time in their young lives. It appears that this is the time when parents go through their own kind of dangerous transition. By now the parents have been together for ten to fifteen years. They may not agree on parenting styles. One is stricter. One is unengaged. One is controlling. One is a pushover and spoils the poor thing. One favors the older child and is hard on the younger child, or vice versa. There may be disagreement in the household about lifestyle. One is messy and doesn't care. One gets fat and won't exercise. One spends way too much money they don't have. One drinks too much or is addicted to prescription drugs. One never comes home until late. One has an Internet boyfriend or girlfriend they won't admit to. One is addicted to sports or online games. One hates sex. One has an important job and family priorities can wait. One won't cook anymore and the other won't say, "Thank you." There is a constant fight over money.

Sometimes they divorce or live apart. The child becomes a *floater.* Can you imagine how that feels, *really?* Sometimes they both want you, and sometimes neither one of them wants you, and then sometimes they only want you if child support is tied to your presence. Or they want you unless they already have a date. Hmmmm. Then come stepbrothers and new family, and new lovers come and go. They don't appear to belong anywhere but they can't just disappear. Or can they (they think)? What if I just run away? I wonder if anyone will notice?

Children who spend hours alone are infinitely more likely to be groomed and recruited by predators.

In a discussion of fantasy relationships, I would be remiss if I did not address the issue that this is not limited to teenagers. It seems like at least once a week, I hear of a couple having trouble in their relationship or are divorcing. One or the other of them is addicted to the Internet or online gaming. Eventually it comes out that they have a "digital date." It is not really love, just friends – really, who are you kidding? These folks are spending more time with their Internet partner than they are with their husband or wife. If this is you, *stop and wake up*. First of all, people are noticing. Second of all, you are living in a fantasy world exactly like the victim above. On the Internet, *everything looks good*. One party lures you in and tells you every-thing you want to hear. Or you are playing "Second Life," and living in a fantasy world. Think about this. In Internet life, you don't do the laundry. You don't have to pay the bills. Everyone appears fabulous, slim, funny and easy to be with. This process is no different than the girl above. He/she can be everything you have always wanted, *but grow up*. They tell you a few things and you fill in the blanks. You are obsessed with your own fantasy. You own it. All of a sudden, your children are a pain. Your husband/wife is fat and smells bad. He/she doesn't understand your needs. He/she won't listen. She won't cook. He/She spends too much money. Sex is boring... hello... sound familiar?

Then you need professional counseling. You are obsessed with your own fantasy. You will ultimately lose the trust and respect of everyone around you. People who leave their wife or husband (even emotionally) because they believe they can do better are in for a lifetime of heartache. You are trying to get your spouse and your children to live up to your fantasy. Trust me, whoever is on the other end is not going to be able to do that either. I would suggest that you get off the Internet and pay attention to what you have before you. Engage. You might be surprised to learn that they have missed you, too. Get professional help and work through your fantasy. It may be that your marriage was in trouble anyway. Trust me; a fantasy relationship is not going to fix what will take hard work, honest dialogue, and give and take. Your children will learn from your behavior and follow your lead and use you as an example for problem solving in their own lives. If all of your complaints start with, "I want," "I need," "I can't stand it," and end with, "They won't," "They don't," "They turn me off," then *you need help.*

Wake up. You are obsessed with your fantasy relationship.

I always find it interesting when I am working with cases of sex trafficking that almost always, the number one seduction used by a predator is that you can be part of "family." It is no accident that the pimp is called, "Daddy," and the girl is called, "Wifey." When children run away and a predator spots a scared, young fourteen-year-old getting off a bus, his first words will be, "Come crash with us. We are one big family, no strings attached." Of course it is a lie. He is telling her what she wants to hear. That is why pimps work in stables. He will constantly reassure the girls that they are his "family," and he is going to take care of them. The truth of course is that she will earn the money and give it to him and she really gets only a small amount to live on. She stays because she wants with all her heart to be "family," and she overlooks the truth and fills in the blanks with her fantasy family.

Children who live a "fragmented" family lifestyle are incredibly vulnerable to being groomed and recruited. Many were previously sexually abused. Many of these children create fantasies of what a family would look like, and dream of someone saving them. It is almost like they are wearing a bill-board for a predator. They fantasize what it would be like to have a real family, so they are easy prey on the Internet to be seduced into believing that a predator who is offering them an exploitative relationship will come to love them once he gets to know them, and it will be real love.

Some psychologists have suggested that the reason a 14-15 year old girl may allow herself to get pregnant is based on the false belief that having her own baby will give her a family that no one can take from her. It is the illusion that this child will always need her and no one can take it away from her and she will never be alone again. Of course we all understand the fallacy of that thinking but it does indicate the depth of the hole in these girl's hearts that make them so vulnerable to a predator.

This line of reasoning creates the hierarchy of vulnerability of potential victims: 1.) Foster children 2.) Homeless children 3). Runaway children 4.) Pregnant teens. Truthfully, *all* children are vulnerable, especially if they are from broken homes or have little adult supervision in their lives. The challenge for law enforcement and parents working with this population is that their very identity, the foundations of their lives that determine trust and belonging, have been damaged and are fragmented. Conducting the exercise that I outlined above might be helpful in breaking through their fantasy, but they have an extremely important added circumstance that makes the exercise a bit challenging.

First they lack trust. They lack security. They lack belief in themselves. The biggest factor of all, being exploited by someone who *pretends* to care about them, might be more supportive and consistent than the environment they are living in. In other words, many of these children have little to return to, so they cling to the lies of the pimps and predators with all their hearts. Only when the relationship gets extremely violent, or he won't let her protect herself with condoms, does she start to allow herself to believe that she has been duped. It is all a lie. This process can take a while.

This is the insidious nature of the work of law enforcement dealing with victims of sex trafficking. Legally they are victims and should not be arrested. There are times law enforcement will hold a victim on other crimes, just to try to buy some time away from the pimp or bottom girl, to talk some sense into them and build their trust. Often law enforcement will bring a young girl in six to eight times before she begins to listen. Until then, she will swear he is her boyfriend, they are in love, they are in business together, or she is just doing it until he gets a job or just so they can pay the rent. She clings to the hope that he really loves her.

In these cases it is extremely difficult to break through the girl's thinking patterns. The challenge is that her life is so unstable and she feels so unloved that she will hang on to an abusive and exploitative relationship because she believes it is better than what she had. It is hard to leave an abusive relationship if the victim cannot visualize a better alternative. This is often the case in working with adults in domestic violence relationships. Just think how much more frightening it is if you are fourteen or fifteen and he has convinced you that you are so ruined, so destroyed, and have so little worth that no one else will want you.

In this case, the exercise above may be valuable to help her see that he is not a knight in shining armor to rescue her. Sometimes if the girl is intelligent, it is helpful to answer the questions in her own words so she is admitting to herself the truth without an outsider grilling her in accusatory tones. This can be helpful, especially if she is in the early stages of being groomed and recruited. However, it is even more critical to spend time to help the girl to see her own value and worth. In these situations, the emphasis needs to be not so much on proving to her that he is not the guy she has fantasized about, but for her to see that she is worth so much more than he will ever give her.

I believe one critical element in reaching at risk youth is to help them to develop a vision of what is possible. I have been working on a concept "Create Yourself" to help kids see that they have the control over their lives if THEY decide to. That they have talent and value and that we believe they can achieve far beyond what they think if we can just help them to imagine it in their mind. This is exciting for them to consider and may be just enough to cause them to question their dependency on their pimp or boyfriend.

Dealing with at-risk children who have already been abandoned, or are torn in a broken home, or who have already been sexually violated, is the work of saints. It might just be the most difficult mission any faith-based organization can take on. It is right on their doorstep. Maybe even sitting in their pews.

I challenge the faith-based community to look around them at their families and their community and realize that if they don't take on this challenge, the moral foundation of our society will be altered forever. It is those children who will father and raise the next generation after them. We must stop and rebuild the foundation of ethics and principles and find the value of each other. I cannot imagine a more important work than the work of helping a young person understand they are a valuable and loved child of God.

CHAPTER EIGHT

THE EPIDEMIC OF SEX TRAFFICKING IN AMERICA

Over *one million children* are trafficked each year throughout the world. That is nearly the size of Dallas or San Diego. Think about that. Children are so vulnerable, they are trusting, sometimes daring, sometimes rebellious, and sometimes they make bad decisions. Sometimes they are not even given the chance to make *any* decision. Today, *one bad decision* can change a child's life forever, and the life of their family.

How bad is the problem in the U.S.? No one knows for sure. The Department of Justice believes that over 300,000 children in the U.S. are victims of human trafficking. We know that almost 1.7 million children per year run away from home and over thirty-five percent of those children will trade their bodies for food or bedding within the first forty-eight hours. We know that gangs are using high school girls to recruit other high school students into prostitution. We believe that as many as fifty percent of pregnant teens not living at home with a stable family are vulnerable to being forced into prostitution. We know that innocent children who would normally never be vulnerable are groomed and recruited through social media and online games and MMORPGs. This is called *human trafficking*.

There is an emerging epidemic in our communities that is extremely disturbing. In some communities and cultures, it threatens to erode the safety and well-being of the neighborhood so that young people are given no choice but to join in or get out of the area. Most of the time, though, it is like cheese in a mousetrap. Innocent children have no idea what they are getting into. Gangs are using their young gang girls and guys to recruit innocent young people into drugs and prostitution, and then they are sold or traded to other gangs – this is human trafficking. Sexual exploitation of our children (human trafficking) is no longer just a one-off. No longer limited to those "throw away children," runaways, homeless, and juvenile delinquents.

In the past few months in Southern California, there have been several large cases where high school children especially were victimized. Four particular cases come to mind. These larger cases take place because the local police join with the FBI and run "reverse stings," targeting ads for prostitutes on backpage.com and craiglist.com. One case rescued 105 children across the U.S., and arrested 150 pimps. In one case around San Diego, they rescued sixty victims of forced prostitution in one night, and many were tattooed with bar codes so the victims would be forced to acknowledge they no longer owned their own bodies. Earlier in 2014, the Long Beach Anti-Human Trafficking Task Force arrested ninety-two pimps and freed twenty-two children ages thirteen to seventeen that were being forced into commercial sexual exploitation. Recently San Diego announced a major bust of a multi-state operation focused on the Tycoon gang, which had joined forces with the Crips. It reiterates what I have spoken about for a long time: gangs are joining forces with cartels and running large-scale prostitution rings. They will victimize anyone they can access, groom, and recruit. In this case there were one hundred victims. One was twelve years old and had been recruited in a San Diego County middle school. Many were teenagers and some were adults. Make no mistake about it: *all were victims* of forced sex trafficking.

Imagine one hundred girls being forced into selling their bodies for money that they do not get to keep. Since I educate children and teachers in schools to prepare them to protect themselves, it occurred to me that one hundred people is the size of *three* high school classrooms. Imagine three classrooms full of girls being sold for sex eight to fifteen times a day, moved from motel to motel, beaten, burned, gang raped, and sodomized (without condoms), and most are controlled by withholding food and being plied with drugs to make them compliant.

As I write this, the FBI just announced a major national bust where 149 teenagers were being sex trafficked and they arrested 153 pimps, many from Los Angeles and outlying areas. But some victims were from Wichita Kansas, Nebraska, Ohio, Texas. Missouri and across the Midwest. It is truly an epidemic.

Today, teenagers, *all teenagers*, are vulnerable to being lured in unsuspectingly by a predator. It is silent, subtle and seductive. In 2012, a full seventy-two percent of all California human trafficking cases involved U.S. citizens. Who is at risk? Our children, your children, children who need money, children with low self-esteem, special needs children, children who are having sex anyway. Children who use the Internet and smartphones. Need I say more?

We all have something in common with these children. *We all want to be loved.* That makes us all vulnerable. Predators recognize children with an intense need to be loved and without the tools to protect themselves. That is why Million Kids wrote The Love Trap and Grace, Hope and Fatherhood. They are designed to be human trafficking prevention programs for parents and teens.

The Love Trap is the basis for understanding human trafficking, including the grooming and recruitment process. It teaches government officials, school administrators, civic leaders, teachers, parents, and teenagers how predators identify a potential victim, the methods they use to recruit innocent children, how parents can recognize the signs that their child is being recruited, and most important, it teaches young people how to protect themselves so they will not become victims of human trafficking. The Love Trap Program has been delivered to over 50,000 individuals. throughout the U.S. to help keep children safe from predators. Currently, volunteers are being trained locally to be able to deliver The Love Trap to schools and civic groups across the U.S.

Million Kids also created Grace, Hope and Fatherhood. This is a program developed as a collaboration between Kerry Decker, pastor, author, artist and international human rights activist, and

Opal Singleton, President of Million Kids, and underwritten through the generosity of Tyndale Publishing. Grace, Hope and Fatherhood is a theologically sound curriculum to assist the faith-based community in developing effective programs to educate and empower parents and teens in how to prevent human trafficking and protect potential victims in their neighborhoods. There are six segments with six videos, study guides and supported by scripture to help the faith-based community understand how to create programs that can educate parents, protect vulnerable societal groups, and educate young people about how predators identify their targets and lure them into sex trafficking. This program can be ordered and downloaded at www.churchaction-network.com.

As I previously mentioned the most likely targets of a predator for grooming and recruitment into minor sex trafficking are: 1.) Foster children, 2.) Homeless children 3.) Runaway children and 4.) Pregnant teens. After that, *all* children are vulnerable if they use social media, video chat rooms, or hookup apps, or play online games or MMORPGs (massive multi-player online role playing games). Statistics vary, but it is believed that nearly sixty percent of teens in prostitution come from the foster care system and nearly eighty percent of homeless children come from the foster care system. The reason foster children are so vulnerable is that they are just like you and me, except we had someone who thought we were the greatest thing since sliced bread and foster children do not. They most likely have been shuffled from home to home, and when they are twelve or thirteen and going through puberty, a smooth-talking older guy will come along and pat them on the head, promise them the moon, make all their dreams come true, and "poof" they are gone. They will be systematically groomed, recruited, and exploited into sex trafficking.

Law enforcement, probation, social services and hundreds of non-profit organizations helping children at risk will expend hours, energy, grief, and concern reaching out to these victims, trying to keep them from "the life" (a term used for prostitution) or trying to get them to leave their pimp and get out of "the life." Once a victim recruited by a *romeo pimp* is in "the life," they will be brought into custody on average six to eight times before they are willing to listen. They have indeed been "groomed." This is the hardest population to work with in helping victims of sex trafficking. They are young and they are groomed and convinced the pimp loves them. They believe they have found a family. They believe with all their hearts that when the chips are down, the pimp will take care of them because they are taking care of him. They often perceive themselves as being in business with him. Or they are just doing this until the rent is paid or until he gets a job. He has groomed them so that they are totally loyal.

The romeo pimp grooming process in prostitution often resembles the domestic violence cycle. It starts with getting the victim to be totally dependent on the pimp and even the *bottom girl* (a girl who works for the pimp) at times. He will learn all of her dreams and fears and build her up. Oftentimes she is quite young—twelve, thirteen, fourteen or even fifteen years old—and he is twenty, twenty-five or even thirty years old.

A common misconception is that pimping is all about sex. That is not accurate. Pimping is about mind control. It is about exploiting another person for power and personal financial gain. The romeo pimp sweet talks a vulnerable young girl, addressing her every fear. In today's society, our children have been raised to be low-hanging fruit. A child who has been raised in foster care or in a dysfunctional broken home appears to be wearing a billboard that reads, "Take me, I need to be loved."

Let me set the record straight. I have met hundreds, even thousands of children from broken homes and foster care that have strong character and are not easy pickings for a predator. I have met nearly as many children from regular homes without supervision who meet the profile of "low-hanging fruit." My point here is that vulnerability and the need to be loved, combined with the appearance of being sexually active, will accelerate a teen right to the top of being a target for a predator.

The romeo pimp process starts with providing a victim with the answer to all her fears and needs. The goal is to put the victim on a pedestal and reinforce her ego. The pimp tries to make her think that he/she believes in her. It is not about the relationship, it is a strategy for gaining control. It is, in fact, true "grooming."

Then the pimp will begin to bring her down. It starts simple at first. For example, they go for ice cream, but she can only have vanilla because chocolate will make her fat. What is that about? He has just decided what she will be allowed to eat. It is the beginning of grooming for control. He begins to pick out her clothes and they don't look like the outfits that she and mom used to shop for. Maybe she gets a small tattoo with his name on it. Then *she* makes him mad. He does not get mad all by himself. It is *her* fault, because she made him mad. Again, it is all about controlling her behavior. She blames herself. She knew if she did that particular thing he would get mad. What was she thinking? She makes up her mind to try harder next time. This is an example of the grooming process within a one-on-one relationship.

Once the grooming process has successfully made the victim completely dependent on the pimp for approval and love, they move into the next phase of recruitment that results in exploitation. Let me be clear, this is a grooming strategy; it is not a failed relationship. It is like setting a hook when catching a fish. The pimp becomes "Daddy" and she is "Wifey." It is all about family and replacing the family that she was disenchanted with before she met him.

He will remind her that they did not love her, but he does. She needs to please him and keep him happy. It is all about *her* performance. She tries harder to prove her loyalty and love. Then he begins to say things like, "Oh, baby, this just makes me sick. I don't want you to have to do 'this,' but I have no choice. I need you to do 'this,' just this one time. I promise never again." When I speak in high schools to young girls, I tell them that if they ever hear those words, pack right then and there and get out. It will never get any better than it is at that one moment. Nothing they can do will change it, except to escape before they become violated. It is a trap. We call it the "Love Trap."

As I have previously suggested, if the victim agrees to have sex just once, then it quickly accelerates into having sex "just with my friends," or "just until the rent is paid," or "just until I get a job." The victim actually begins to see herself in business with him. She is proving her loyalty. He loves her and this is just temporary. In case after case that I have known about, the victim will be picked up for prostitution, drugs, shoplifting, or other crimes six to eight times before she begins to realize that she is just another prostitute in his stable. The domination, control, and ownership accelerate. She is trapped in a cycle of acceptance and rejection by the pimp, and being controlled and disciplined by the bottom girl. It is reminiscent of the domestic violence cycle of reward and punishment, acceptance and rejection, with the victim trying harder and harder to please in the hope of being allowed to stay.

The cases with young victims who have been groomed by a romeo pimp are extremely challenging for law enforcement and Child Protective Services. On the one hand, they are victims, and on the other hand they are perpetrators as they will continue shoplifting, recruiting other innocent teens into the life, and they are most often drug-addicted. It is a complex issue as the victims alternate between being victim and perpetrator. They have been truly "groomed," and most will hang on tightly to their dream that the pimp truly loves them and he will rescue them and keep them safe. As time goes on and the quality of their lives deteriorates, he may begin to beat them, lock them in a closet, burn them with cigarettes, and ultimately he will require them to have sex without a condom. Most girls realize that having sex with multiple customers a day without a condom is in fact, a death sentence. It may finally occur to her that he does not care if she lives or dies. She is replaceable. Sometimes this is a breaking point for victims if authorities have picked them up and a deputy or law enforcement officer has begun to build a trust relationship. However, it is difficult. One would hope that at some point young girls would realize that if they were being forced to have sex without protection, he really does not care if they live or die. That is not always the case.

The other kind of grooming and recruitment that we often see in child sex trafficking cases is called g*orilla pimping*. I have also seen it called guerilla pimping, and I think that might be more descriptive of the actual violation. In street language it is called "gorilla pimping". As I have said before this often times involves what is known as a "bottom girl". A bottom girl is usually eighteen to thirty years old and started young in a stable (as a prostitute). She has worked her way up the ladder to become the pimp's right hand girl. In Southern California, the average age for entering into prostitution is just under thirteen years old. That means that a bottom girl who is probably eighteen to twenty-four is experienced and has proven her loyalty to the pimp or gang. The pimp will put her in charge of recruiting, discipline, placing ads on backpage.com and craigslist.com and oftentimes she manages the money. This is not a hobby for a bottom girl. Her survival depends on it. She *must* recruit new victims or she will be demoted and put back out on the street herself. She is motivated to produce new recruits and make sure they perform. Gangs particularly favor using bottom girls for recruiting victims into sex trafficking. If you follow Million Kids (Riverside) on Facebook, where we routinely post new cases several times a day, you will be amazed that nearly every case of forced prostitution involved another woman. It will not necessarily identify this woman as a bottom girl, but now you are informed and you will recognize her role.

In many cases across the country, gangs have actually placed bottom girls in high schools for the sole purpose of recruiting other girls into prostitution. That is why Million Kids spends so much time educating school administrators, teachers, counselors, school psychologists, nurses, and security personnel to be able to recognize if potential grooming and solicitation might be taking place. It is subtle and difficult to spot. However, by recognizing the process and being aware of the situation, school officials might be able to spot it. That is also why I train the students and the parents so they can overcome the naivety of an innocent-appearing relationship with a newfound girlfriend. The grooming and recruitment process is quick (often under two weeks) as the bottom girl is pressured to produce new recruits. This process is insidious in that most parents, grandparents and even school administrators are expecting a pimp (recruiter) to be a male.

The bottom girl will identify a vulnerable target and make friends through schools and malls, and the grooming process usually is accelerated by texting, tweeting, meeting on Kik, posting on Instagram or Facebook, and building a new friendship. Most parents are oblivious as to the nature of the relationship. Once the relationship is solidified, the bottom girl may take a potential target to a party and get her to engage in illicit sex. It is filmed and then the film is later used to threaten the girl with posting the photos on Facebook, and passing them around to friends and family unless she agrees to engage in prostitution even while living at home. This is called "sextortion".

Sometimes the bottom girl convinces the young girl since she is having sex anyway, why not turn a few tricks with her and have a little fun and pick up some easy money. The victim is usually naïve and uninformed, and is like a lamb being led to slaughter. She is totally unable to comprehend she has started down a path that she cannot escape. That is why the work of Million Kids and other organizations that train in schools is so important. It is critical that young people learn how this works before they are sucked in.

I recently sat with a grandmother whose granddaughter had a new older girlfriend. The granddaughter was getting her hair done, new nails, and was recently found with a roll of money. The grandmother was suspicious as it appeared odd, but she had not yet been educated about the grooming and recruitment process. That evening (Saturday), the new girlfriend had already purchased a ticket to take her granddaughter to Universal Studios. As we talked, the grandmother realized that her granddaughter was most likely being groomed and recruited by a bottom girl. I counseled the grand-mother to take the girl out of town herself or out to dinner, a movie or anything where she sat side-by-side with her all night. This girl was already deep into the grooming process and I suspect that if the girl had gone to Universal Studios with her new "girlfriend," then most likely she would not be seen again.

Gorilla pimping does not always have to include a bottom girl, but it is my cursory estimation based on real cases that at least sixty percent of this type of recruitment involves another girl. That number is not scientific, and I suspect the estimation is much higher, even up to eighty percent of the quick recruitment methodologies. Gorilla pimping is especially brutal and often results in the victim being sold or turned over to gangs.

One of the reasons I have written this book is because I want the readers to see just how quickly a groomed and recruited innocent life can turn into a nightmare. The gorilla pimping process is exceptionally brutal. In romeo pimping, it can take place over a long time and gently ease the victim into "the life" based on a romantic relationship. The gorilla pimping process often happens quickly and so the grooming process is quite short, often under two weeks. Rather than coaxing compliance, the girl will be turned over to a gang or a gorilla pimp, and to gain compliance they will be put the victim through a brutal and disgusting breaking process. They usually will be removed from the geographical location they are familiar with, so if they break free they will not know where they are or how to get home. They are often drugged and gang raped and gang sodomized. They may be locked in a closet for several days so they humiliate themselves, and withholding food controls them. They may be branded with a tattoo. They are degraded verbally and physically. They are often filmed so they can be marketed on the Internet. They are often filmed in sex acts and forced to watch. They are constantly told they have lost all value as a woman and human being and that no one else will ever want them. They are convinced they cannot go back to their old lives.

In gorilla pimping, the pimp (and/or bottom girl) will often collect information on the victim during the grooming process. Sometimes it is through a fraudulent job application, or postings on the Internet, or just through friendships with the bottom girl. They will use that information to threaten the girl with killing her family, or making her little sister a prostitute, or forcing her brother into a gang. These threats are real and sometimes reinforced with waving guns and knives.

I read of an extremely sad case this past year in Yorba Linda, California, where a beautiful and intelligent young lady was murdered. She was a 4.0 student, and she wanted to become an attorney. Her parents were successful and prominent in the community. Somehow, this exceptional young lady fell in love with a romeo pimp and he brutalized her terribly. At one point it is said that he beat her with a tire iron. She got free and went into a safe house. Somehow a message was sent to her (probably by a bottom girl) that if she did not get out of there and return to him, he would kill her entire family. She felt responsible for them and was afraid. She left the safe house and returned to him. He killed her. My heart bleeds for her family.

To an uninformed, uninvolved person it is difficult to understand the levels of depravity, violence, and abuse that some of these trafficked victims are subjected to. Most pimps are deviant sociopaths who exhibit no empathy or concern for their victims. It is all about power, control, and greed.

Contrast that with the image of a pimp that our media and music portray to our young people. Rap music, YouTube, and movies all glorify pimps and hos. The Miley Cyrus song, "Morning Sun" (pimps and hos) YouTube video received over 660,000 hits. There are TV shows called "Pimp My Ride."

To the teen culture, pimps and hos are no big deal. In fact, many idolize the concept. Need I point out that this book is called *Seduced: The Grooming of America's Teenagers?* Our young people have been seduced into believing that pimps and hos are a cool thing and nothing to fear. From this perspective, it is a short distance between locating a rebellious thirteen-year-old girl posting sexy photos on the web and grooming her to believe that she is special and he is going to take her places and introduce her to the life of her dreams. Like a fly trapped in a web, there is no way out.

Oftentimes, the girl is quickly hooked on drugs, but not always. Some pimps revel in controlling by psychological manipulation and don't want to lose money on supplying a girl's drug habit. Regardless of the process, just try to imagine how quickly a young girl's life can change. One week she is mad at mom because she cannot go to a particular party, and the next week she is trapped in a closet, trying to recover from a gang rape.

It is my mission. Every day I get up vowing that never again should this happen to our young people. It is a trap. I call it The Love Trap. All it takes is one bad decision and the life of a child and their family can be changed forever. If you tell the young people how this works, they will listen. I know. I do that nearly seven days a week. I drive over 40,000 miles a year and try to raise money as I go. If you want to help by donating, go to www.millionkids.org.

Human trafficking of our children is not inevitable.

If it is a crime of psychology, then education is the key. If everyone who reads this book shares it with five more people, then we can begin to make the changes within our society that will start to inform parents, grandparents, and teens and keep our young people safe. Knowledge is power when shared.

One of the reasons that human trafficking is the fastest growing crime in America is because gangs have found both teen and adult prostitution to be especially lucrative. In San Diego on January 27, 2014, the *San Diego Union Tribune* ran an article that quoted the FBI as saying, "Sex Trafficking Overtakes Drugs as San Diego Gang's Top Cash Source." That means in San Diego, gangs are making more money selling sex than they are selling drugs. Law enforcement will normally tell you that gangs make the most money selling 1.) Guns; 2) Drugs; 3.) Sex. Gangs know they can sell drugs once and guns once, but that they can sell people over and over. To sell guns or drugs, you obtain a load of merchandise and sell it and then it needs to be replaced. People can be sold endlessly. If a gang is picked up by law enforcement with a load of illegal guns, they go to prison. If a gang is picked up with a vanload of girls, it looks like a party.

Let's do the math regarding prostitution to help you understand just how lucrative sex trafficking is for gangs. Your average pimp will have five girls in a "stable." We recently had a case with seven girls, and sometimes there are only three girls belonging to a pimp. Most often the number is five. If each girl makes on average $180,000 a year (average five times a night) for her pimp and each pimp has five girls, then that makes each pimp worth $900,000 to gangs and drug cartels.

Truthfully, most girls have an $800 night quota (eight times) in Southern California, so it is easy to see why gangs and drug cartels are making this the fastest growing crime in the U.S. In many areas of the U.S., gangs are having gang wars over sex trafficking territory. This is similar to the drug wars in the past where every primary drug-selling corner in the U.S. is owned and controlled by a gang. This business is so lucrative that we are actually seeing rival gangs that have undergone severe turf wars in the past, joining forces to be able to capitalize on sex trafficking territory. The difference is, it is youth that are the commodity that is being accessed, groomed, recruited, and sold.

In my experience working with real cases of sex trafficking, the predator has a hierarchy of criteria that they use to evaluate how easy a person might be to groom and recruit.

1. Do they appear to be sexually active? If you are having sex anyway, then you are easier to groom and recruit because you have already crossed a threshold of sex = love. Or at least that is your belief. It is true that many young people flaunt free love. Or treat sex as a recreational choice. The perception they share is that true love requires no return. They are young and it is my experience they will learn the high price of promiscuity is disease, abandonment, and exploitation.

2. Do they need love? Or are they needy? Do they want to be taken care of? Are they looking for someone to rescue them?

3. Do they need money or will they be attracted to the prospect of making easy money?

Think about this criterion. That includes almost all of us. We all like to be loved and few of us have enough money for everything we want. So why does that work on some potential recruits and not others? I believe the answer is in how much you believe in yourself and whether you are seeking approval through sex. In this day of promiscuity and recreational sex, a significant percentage of our teens are sexually active. If you doubt that, then ask yourself why so many states have provided abortions for minors and many provide abortions without needing the consent of an adult. Once you have crossed the threshold of becoming sexually active, then change in attitude is inevitable based on the success of that relationship.

Think about the movie "Pretty Woman," and the message this sends to our girls. By the way, this was a great movie with excellent acting and the critics have acclaimed it for years. In that movie, Julia Roberts "makes love" with Richard Gere for $3,000. Note they "make love," not some sort of kinky perversion that many johns expect when paying a prostitute for services. After they "make love," Julia Roberts is so good in bed (at least that is what they want you to believe) that she ends up shopping on Rodeo Drive and he marries her. Talk about a pipe dream. I have been in the anti-sex trafficking business for nearly seven years, and I have not yet seen a case where a prostitute was paid $3,000, and few of them "make love," but then again I don't live in Hollywood.

Think about your average fifteen-year -old. She is having sex anyway, so why not get paid for it? Maybe she can't get $3,000, but she might get $200 (trust me, they quickly settle for $60). I believe that most young girls think that sex equals love (as it should), but outside a committed relationship, it is simply not true.

I believe our society and even our parenting have not addressed sufficiently the issue of value and respect in a relationship. We live in an artificial, throw away, trial and error world. Anything goes. I think the concept of personal value and self-respect will become even more devaluated as we expose our children to animated sex. Anything is possible in animation. It is not a give and take relationship between two caring adults who understand each other and meet each other's needs. In virtual sex, anything is possible, and commitment or the needs or desires of others are not relevant. It is in essence, virtual masturbation. Yes, you may get the physical release, but you have not engaged in a relationship. There has not been an exchange of emotions.

Let me return to the idea of why being sexually active makes you vulnerable to a predator. Once a teen has engaged in sex and it did not result in a commitment that leaves the young person feeling alternately devalued and defensive of their decision, as they justify that it was no big deal, it was just recreational sex. It is a small leap to "Hey, you are doing it anyway, so why not make some money?" Trust me—the pimps and bottom girls have this concept down pat. Sadly, this is really true if a young person has been previously sexually molested. Especially if they have not been able to get counseling for the trauma they experienced. It is believed that as many as seventy percent of sex trafficking victims were previously sexually molested.

We have an extremely sad case in our community of a fifteen-year-old who disappeared. She later appeared in an undercover video by a local television station doing a feature on prostitution in Tijuana. The story goes that someone came to the girl and said, "You can leave on Friday night and be home on Sunday night and you can pick up $500 and no one will ever know what you did." She fell for it, and the last time she was seen was on the undercover video from Tijuana. We do not know if she is still alive. In the interview, the girl said, "Please tell the kids back home not to fall for this." This beautiful, highly intelligent girl made one bad decision based on the fact that she was having sex anyway, why not have some fun and make some money? It is all a lie!

One of the most vulnerable teenage targets for sex traffickers is a runaway teenager. It is estimated that over 1.69 million children run away a year in the U.S., and literally one out of three of them will be coerced into sex trafficking (prostitution) within the first forty-eight hours. They are extremely easy targets. Pimps and predators can spot a needy, intimidated teen in search of refuge a mile away. They will approach the teen, chitchat for a while, and then tell them they can come crash with their friends because they are all like "family." Guaranteed no strings attached. They will place the scared and needy teenager next to an older woman who will reassure her that she made $500 last night and so can our girl. The terrified girl thinks, "I do not want to do this, but it is only one night and it is $500 and that could last me for the rest of the month." They will never tell her that she does not get to keep the money. In fact, that is one of the biggest lies of all.

It has long been my dream to purchase one thousand billboards across America to say, "Hey girls, listen up: the prostitute never gets the money." In case after case, working with law enforcement, we will see that the girl is controlled by keeping her broke. The girl will earn $500. In fact, she will earn that each night or she does not get to eat or her pimp will beat her. Once she earns the money, he may give her five dollars for a Del Taco and he keeps the rest to buy a fancy pair of shoes, recruit another girl, and pay off a gang or drug cartel. It is all a lie. The girl has been groomed and recruited with little effort. There is nothing more vulnerable than a fifteen-year-old girl who is pregnant without a support system. Pimps and predators prey on their needs including the need for financial income to support the child, the need to have diapers and formula. The pimp will threaten to place the newborn in the system and consistently pressure the girl to prostitute herself to get the income to get her child back out of the system. It is true enslavement. Without a solid support system, pregnant teens are easy to groom and recruit into a life of prostitution.

What about other teenagers? Far too often, I have sat with parents of a teen who was tricked or seduced into exploitation. It takes place in a vast array of methodologies, but the result is the same— boy or girl, guy or gal—pimps and predators identify the victim through peers, in malls, at schools and more than seventy percent of the time the grooming and recruitment is done through social media.

The risk is higher for young people who use smartphones, texting, tweeting, using chat rooms where they are correspondingly more exposed to opportunities to connect with strangers. Additionally, an analysis of many child sex trafficking cases indicates that the predators will comb through Instagram, Facebook, Flickr, Tinder, Kik and other social media sites that post photos. Predators historically seek out individuals who appear in photos as if they are sexually provocative or sexually active. This is the single biggest criterion for grooming and recruiting by most pimps. Predators have a profile they are seeking. Sexually active young people are much more likely to consider prostitution as another form of casual sex, as they are having sex anyway, so why not get paid for it? Of course, this is not universally true across the board, but in many sex trafficking cases that I am familiar with, the greatest portion of victims had had a previous sexual encounter.

So that is the targeting process. Once a potential prey is identified, the predator will then begin to weave a trail of their social media activity. They may meet in a random video chat room or on Tinder, a teen and adult dating site, and then go over to Kik to continue a "sexting" relationship. Young people who meet acquaintances and strangers s on sites like Omegle and ooVoo are more likely to live on the edge. Their parents are not home a lot, perhaps it is a broken home or a child raised by a relative, and often they are latch key kids (children whose parents both work and the teens are deemed too old for a sitter and they are left without guidance, support or supervision). These young people get lonely and bored and in their mind, it is no big deal. They are just having fun. Just goofing off. They are truly easy pickings.

The predator especially looks for young people who post sexually provocative photos/videos, those who are willing to talk about sex with total strangers and young people who use excessive foul language indicating rebellion and a willingness to take risks. Predators look for youth who are vulnerable to seduction and appear to have a "feel" for particularly vulnerable targets of children and teens that have a history of sexual or physical abuse. A conversation will often start with, "How old are you?" "What do you look like?" "Where do you go to school?" or "What is your bra size?"

A common tactic used by predators is to pretend to be another teen on social networking sites. It is a strategy being executed to win trust and appear harmless. The ultimate goal is to build a trusting relationship that will end in a meeting for sex or grooming them for prostitution.

According to the *Journal for Adolescent Health* Vol 47 (2010), in eighty-two percent of online sex crimes against minors, the offender used the victim's social networking site to gain information about the victim's likes and dislikes. Sixty-five percent of online sex predators used the victim's social networking site to gain home and school information about the victim. Twenty-six percent of online sex offenders used the victim's social networking site to gain information about the victim's whereabouts at a specific time.

One in five young people between ten and seventeen years of age have reported receiving an unwanted sexual solicitation online, according to a study done by the Crimes Against Children Research Center at the University of New Hampshire. This same study found that in terms of risk, girls and older youth (fourteen to seventeen years old) were more likely to be solicited according to the recent study publication in *The Journal of the American Medical Association*. According to netsmartz.org, one out of three teens (twelve to seventeen) has experienced online harassment.

A discussion about sex trafficking cannot be complete without informing the reader about how the victim is marketed and sold as a prostitute. Prostitution has been revolutionized because of the Internet. Until recently, streetwalkers would stroll up and down the "blade" or "track," a known location in nearly every town in America. Johns would drive up and down and select a girl (or guy) and make an offer. It was easy to observe and law enforcement from time to time would conduct stings or place girls undercover to arrest the johns. Obtaining specific services for strange and perverted services required the john to negotiate with the selected prostitute, and some were willing and some were not. The Internet has streamlined the process and taken it underground.

Today, most marketing and transactions are negotiated on the Internet. Websites like craigslist.com, and backpage.com make ordering a prostitute nearly as easy as ordering a customized pizza, hold the anchovies. The pimp or bottom girl will photograph the girl. If she is underage, they may provide only photos that do not show the face. They will often use terms like "young" and "fresh". Don't get me wrong. Girls of *all* ages are being promoted on these websites, but with some effort you can easily locate girls who appear to be much younger than the eighteen years old they are promoting. To find this on the web, just go to the particular website, look at your location, select "escort" under "adult services" and then agree to their terms. It is as easy as that to find who is for sale tonight in your town.

Many of these ads will have headlines like "New in Town" or "Last Night in Town" or "Leaving Town

Soon." Most will offer specific kinds of services; many of these are in code. That allows the purchaser to select more customized services that are hard to find. The bottom girl typically has placed the ads on these sites. Often when arrested, the pimp will swear he was never involved and that the victim worked as an independent and placed her own ad. They use gift cards to pay for the ads and will use prepaid cell phones for the telephone number in the ad listing. Heads up, moms and dads, if your kid comes home with a disposable cell phone and a stack of pre-paid gift cards, I would start to ask some questions. It may be a clue they are being recruited.

Let me explain how this works. A girl is groomed, recruited, broken and forced into the life. She will be taken from town to town and placed in a motel. The ads are placed on the website. "New in Town." The Pimp tweets out to existing customers. They take calls and texts for new customers. As a john (sex buyer), you will be booked into room twenty-six from 2:00 to 3:00 P.M. Someone else books room twenty-six from 3:00 to 4:00 P.M... Etc., etc. Much of the time, the girl does not know what town she is in or even what name she is being sold under. She will be in that motel for a couple of days and then moved to the next town, where it starts over again.

To give you an idea how serious this is, I often use photos of girls being sold in the town where I am speaking for the evening. One photo I have used several times is a beautiful young lady with the title, "Leaving Temecula Soon" (a town in California). A while back, I spent many hours looking on the websites for a particular fourteen-year-old who was missing. This is a hobby I have if I have any time or energy left at the end of the day. I searched backpage. com for this girl throughout all of California, Oregon, and Nevada, and could not find her. However, I found "Leaving Temecula Soon" was also being advertised as "Leaving Bakersfield soon" and "Leaving Long Beach Soon." The bottom line is that these girls are on a "sex circuit." They are moved from town to town and often their names are changed.

Whenever I share this information with the public, the same questions always arise and I am sure that you the reader will also have these questions.

1. Why don't they shut down backpage.com, craigslist.com, sipsap.com and any other site that is selling prostitution services? Certainly prostitution is illegal in most states, and so it should be an easy matter. Not necessarily. It is in fact a complex matter. Initially I was on a real warpath to close down backpage. com. For me it was basically the electronic

auctioning of our teenager's (and adults') bodies. My friends at the FBI gave me a different perspective. As long as they are being advertised, we can look for missing people and have some chance of finding them. Backpage.com has been cooperative with law enforcement much of the time. They can help a rescued girl build her case against a pimp. In 2014, My Redbook was shut down by law enforcement. They were notoriously pornographic in their marketing and not cooperative with law enforcement. When you shut down a website like myredbook.com or backpage.com, they will simply go off shore and it will be impossible to secure the necessary documentation to build a case. Even worse, the girls will be even more violated as third world countries will exploit the pornographic photos of the girl worldwide. As long as backpage.com continues to operate, not only can we often track missing girls to build cases, law enforcement can run reverse stings. It is through the reverse sting process that law enforcement has made large-scale arrests such as the cases in Long Beach, California, where they arrested ninety-two pimps over a reasonably short period of time.

The challenge with working with backpage. com and craigslist.com using reverse stings is that the pimps will often not send out the younger girls you are ordering through the ad. That can make it difficult to get access to the young girls being violated.

2. Why don't they run? Almost every time I speak, someone usually asks why a girl stays in the life. This is an important question and even a more important answer to understand. Most of you reading this book are probably adults. That means you are potential jurors. I hope if any of you ever sit on a jury on a sex trafficking case, you will remember this book. Most jurors will say something like, "This girl is in a motel room with an adult male, why doesn't she ask for help in escaping?" First, statistics indicate that most men who are purchasing sex will not want to get involved and help the girl. They want their service delivered and they are out of there before they get caught. The biggest factor, though, has to do with brainwashing, conditioning, and grooming. If the girl has been groomed by a romeo pimp, she believes that she is pleasing her "Daddy." Even if he is beating her, burning her, locking her up or making her

work eighteen hours in a day, she is still trying to get his approval. He is manipulating her with an alternating cycle of acceptance and rejection. Most likely though, the girls on the circuit are victims of gorilla pimping. They are being held under the worst circumstances. They will be tortured in despicable ways that are not fit to describe in a public book. They are often threatened with guns, knives, and killing of family members. If they are in gang trafficking, they will be forced to service the gang after a long night of making their quota with the public. Withholding food and being plied with drugs often controls them. Only after a girl has reached a point where she is able to understand that she will probably die if she does not get out of the life will she begin to find ways to try to get help. If she is caught trying to get help or escape the life, she could be killed in inhumane ways. The truth. There is no good answer. If you ever see a girl trying to get help, please, please, contact your human trafficking task force or call the police. She may only get one chance.

3. What about the demand side of this equation? What happens to the johns who are the buyers of sex? If there were no demand,

there would be no sellers. Well, now you have a point there. No buyer, then no need for a seller. It is not as easy as it appears. Research tells us that traditionally the sex buyer is around thirty-eight years old and more than half are in a committed relationship. Hmmm. Part of the issue is that most johns think of it as prostitution as usual. I often hear that prostitution is the oldest profession in the world and so I need to get a grip. However, these guys are not aware that things have changed dramatically. Certainly, until recent history, a girl could decide to be an independent prostitute. Some worked with pimps and were abused and many worked independently. However, with gangs and drug cartels entering the arena, it is a whole new world.

With sex trafficking being more lucrative for gangs and drug cartels, we have gang warfare to claim lucrative sex trafficking territories. That makes it harder and harder for an independent prostitute to operate without paying a fee to a gang. Even more important, a john needs to be educated on the changes taking place. Think about this. If a gang is willing to groom and recruit a fifteen-year-old girl and exploit her beyond description, then a gang will think nothing of arranging to take photos of the sex acts with the prostitute without the john's knowledge and then extort thousands of dollars from him to keep it away from his wife and his employer.

One of the reasons that I often give nearly three hundred presentations a year to the public, churches, and government officials is to help educate men to understand the real dangers and potential destruction that comes from the idea that prostitution is harmless and is a private matter. Not only is some-body's daughter being violated and exploited, but he could easily find that he is also about to become the victim of a gang or drug cartel. Hopefully, just that knowledge will be enough to make the average man think twice before committing one of the most compromising acts possible.

All of this is based on the idea of the "average" john. Certainly arresting johns and having them pay a price is helpful in most states. However, in California it is simply a misde-meanor. By the time law enforcement issues a citation, the john is long gone on his way and the poor police officer is stuck with an hour-and-a-half of paperwork that keeps him from saving the lives of others in need. I believe the answer is two-fold. Educate the john about the danger he is placing himself in and the violation taking place with his "date," and also increase the penalty for soliciting sex.

A discussion of johns would not be complete without exploring the concept of shaming johns to stop them from ever purchasing sex from a prostitute again. There is a strong trend with district attorney offices throughout the nation to place the photo of sex buyers on Internet web sites and even billboards. Certainly shame can be a deterrent. As an activist, I have mixed emotions about this process. Personally, I favor the concept of "john schools" being conducted in fifty-two cities across the U.S. These are first offender court-ordered diversion programs that can provide the john with the opportunity to erase the arrest once he has completed a one or two-day school. Typically, the school's curriculum includes information about sex trafficking, diseases, laws, and victim exploitation. Sometimes the johns are referred to additional resources where they can get counseling, etc.

The reason I favor this is that I believe that in most cases, shaming a man will not help if he is dealing with a sexual addiction or compulsion. The other reason I am against billboards and john postings on websites is that the victim most likely has a family. If their fifteen-year-old son or daughter passes a billboard with dad's photo on it for solicitation of a prostitute and they have their friends with them on their way to school, then you have several more innocent victims. So for first offenders, I believe education and counseling referral will have a greater chance of changing behavior than a public shaming approach. However, if we are talking about a second offense or more, then throw the book at them. I personally will help post their photos.

Let me offer one final thought about johns. Because prostitution is changing, I believe we will see a change in the profile of the john. I believe as more and more gangs enter into sex trafficking, you will see more and more gang johns, and in those cases all the shaming and education in the world will probably not stop the prostitution activity.

I am often asked the question: If we legalize prostitution, won't that eliminate sex trafficking? My opinion is *"no."* Take a look at Nevada, where prostitution is legal in some counties. Nevada is on the sex trafficking circuit for almost every serious pimp. When large-scale events are held in Nevada, pimps organize hundreds, maybe thousands of prostitutes to come in from all over the U.S. The planning and logistics are equal to many corporations. It is similar to stories you hear about the Super Bowl and other large-scale events. Legalizing simply drives demand, and that means they need girls to be brought in to maximize the profits. Legalizing prostitution does not mean that the recruitment and treatment of the girls will be improved. The pimps want to make money any way they can and they are not going to suddenly become nice and treat the girls like princesses just because it is now legal. Again, pimping is not about sex. It is about power, mind control and making money.

CHAPTER NINE

CHILD PORNOGRAPHY, DIGITAL EXPLOITATION AND TEEN PORN ADDICTION

Most experts who deal with human trafficking understand that there are more girls being sex trafficked than guys. Certainly the proportions of guys being violated increase when you talk about sex trafficking within the LBGT (Lesbian, Gay, Bisexual, and Transgender) community. That has more to do with promiscuity and having multiple partners before settling down, which several of my LBGT friends tell me is the case. The more exposure you have to multiple relationships, the greater the odds that you will encounter a predator looking to exploit the vulnerable and those wanting to be loved. There is an additional factor in the LBGT community and that is a situation where young people are often thrown out of the home when a family member discovers they may be gay. That often forces the young person into the streets and may result in their becoming homeless and extremely vulnerable to exploitation. Quite frankly, there is not enough attention being given to trafficking and exploitation in the LBGT community. There is a dire need for leadership to create programs for outreach and counseling.

In prostitution most of the exploited are girls with a ratio of about 5 to 1 girls to guys being exploited. Males are more likely to be......Guys are more likely to be exploited by being coerced into sending a naked or sexually engaged photo to what they believe is a girl, but it turns out to be a man connected to a large-scale child porn ring. The photo is then passed from pervert to pervert, and sometimes the male victim will receive masses of emails from men wanting to have sex with him. This is especially traumatic to guys who perceive themselves as heterosexual and realize they have been duped. The emails are often accompanied with blackmail or sextortion, and the trapped guy begins to panic as he becomes aware that his photo is going around the world on a child porn ring, *forever*, with no way to get it back. That scenario can be extremely damaging to a teen male's self-esteem.

The Internet has brought a vast amount of changes in how child porn rings operate. A few years ago, a kiddy porn addict would subscribe to underground magazines, find a few friends in foreign countries who lived on the margins, or purchase their child porn from large porn studios in Los Angeles. The World Wide Web has streamlined the activity and greatly expanded the reach to child porn perverts. Today with the advances in technology, most child pornographers have web cams and make their own. However, they need a child, so they use their own children or grandchildren, borrow a niece or nephew, or coerce a neighbor's child. Sometimes they will go to foster agencies and bring home a foster child. I will share with you some sickening statistics, but I think it is important that we understand just how vile kiddy porn is. Research statistics indicate that approximately thirty-nine percent of children being exploited as victims of child pornography manufacturers are under the age of five and about nineteen percent are under the age of two. This should make all hearts bleed.

Additionally, the laws have changed in some states to make the manufacturing and distribution of child pornography a part of human trafficking. In California, until Proposition 35 passed, manufacturing and distributing was not classified as human trafficking. Now it is. I always thought it was. Truthfully, to make child pornography, you need a *child*. To be pornographic you need to exploit that child. Not all cases of child pornography in California result in a human trafficking charge. However, when a perpetrator uses force, fraud or coercion in the act of making or distributing child pornography, it can result in a charge of human trafficking depending on the circumstances.

So now we have tens of thousands of people (mostly men) making their own child pornography. The Internet is expanding in speed and reach, almost beyond description. It is this capability that has allowed the creation of large-scale child porn rings around the world. Many are operated on the Tor Network, a large-scale complex network system designed to improve participants' privacy and security. Private porn rings are formed in very secret global rings and sub-rings, where they are able to validate the identity of the participant to try to avoid being penetrated by law enforcement. In July 2014, the largest child porn ring in the world was busted by federal authorities and it allegedly had 27,000 child pornography subscribers. It boggles my mind to imagine how much pornographic material is required to keep 27,000 kiddie porn perverts satisfied. Twenty-seven-year-old Jonathan Johnson from Abita Springs, Louisiana, allegedly operated it. The site was used by predators to "convince or coerce children into sending them sexually explicit videos," according to wbrz.com news. Most of the victims were guys. Interestingly enough, there was a sub-ring of women child pornographers, and later a forty-year-old woman from San Diego was arrested with 40,000 images of child pornography. As the stories unfolded, it became apparent that many of the men in the child porn ring would pose as girls or women, and therefore were able to get their victims to send a photo of themselves in all their naked glory.

Think about this situation as if this was your thirteen-year-old son who has been duped and is now being blackmailed. How can he tell anyone he has been tricked? How can he get the photos back? He can't. NEVER! The photos have most likely gone out to tens of thousands of men and women who have probably traded them for images of other children. His photo is going around and around the globe to be drooled over by child perverts, and this young man has no way to reverse this. Imagine the shame. Imagine the panic. I know, because I get calls from young people trying to get the photos back. It is impossible.

An extremely critical point – please stop and think this through with me. *In some ways, this guy is as emotionally exploited as the girl who has been physically abused.* He will panic. He will think of suicide. He will not be able to talk to anyone about it. He feels violated. He is ruined. He plays football. What if the guys find out? If word gets out, he will be bullied. What if it ends up with some other young person's dad and they recognize him? What if *his* dad finds out? Then here they come. His text number was on the photo. He begins to get hundreds of offers from men around the globe wanting to have sex with him. Some are graphic. Some want to meet him. Some may live in the same town as him. He is heterosexual. He feels dirty. He thinks he is ruined.

I would submit that this young man needs the same kind of non-judgmental intervention as we recommend for girls who have been trafficked. First, most guys will never come forward and admit their abuse. Somehow it appears to violate their self-image of being manly. They berate themselves for being stupid. They think a real man would know better.

I recommend that parents read this concept carefully and give it some thought. Detecting shame-based behavior in males is harder, but intervention is extremely critical. Usually the signs involve emotion-ally shutting down, retreating to online games, going into isolation, and erupting or suppressed anger.

He might even break up with his girlfriend. Professional counselors can be most helpful, but first a parent needs to be sensitive enough to rec-ognize there is a change in behavior. Remember this event is probably not a one-time email and it is over. The offers will continue and it will be difficult for him to access his normal apps and websites and texts without re-violation. Even if he is not willing to talk, it is important to reassure him that whatever he is dealing with, you are there for him. This is especially valuable to hear from another male. If you cannot come up with another helpful intervention, at least remember the most important gift you can give another human being is to say, "I believe in you."

Another alternative is to find activities away from the Internet. Select activities that the teen is good at. Maybe running, fishing, basketball, go carting, or whatever. The point is to get him out away from the computer and work on rebuilding his self-esteem. Perhaps then he will open up. Perhaps not. At least he knows he is not alone and you have his back.

What about the teen that becomes addicted to pornography himself (or herself)? Youth ministers are telling me that more and more teens are starting to admit to having a serious pornography addiction. This is no surprise. Internet pornography has few limitations. It is often carefully introduced in games and social media sites. Children are experiencing nudity, sex acts, and vulgar language at extremely young ages. As I discussed in the Numbing Down chapter, there appears to be little or no sensitivity to what we used to call porn. In pubescent teens sorting through sexual identity, this can be especially damaging. It is easy for parents, especially dads, not to take this seriously. Certainly normal curiosity is to be expected. However, if a teen were exhibiting signs of changing behavior or evidence of accessing sites that could be considered pornographic, I would advise that the teen be introduced to a professional outside counselor.

In my time spent with David Stewart, Riverside LMFT who specializes in pornography and sex addiction, he has shared with me that the younger people are when exposed to pornography, the more likely they are to become a victim or act out as a perpetrator and become addicted to pornography themselves.

Somehow, our society does not take seriously the collateral damage done to young people when they are exposed to pornography or are abused at a young age. In my opinion, it is a ticking time bomb, especially with boys. I recently read of an exceptional pediatrician in the Midwest who is going to prison for possession of child pornography. He appeared like an absolutely great guy. Just the kind of guy you would want to take your children to see. He was not making child pornography or distributing, but he had viewed it and kept it. He was in a position of public trust as a medical doctor and so he needed to pay a higher price. What caught my attention was his statement that he had been molested as a young child and he had never taken the time to deal with it. He believed he was acting on his unresolved impulses. That is absolutely no excuse. However, I admire the man to understand that if a person (male or female) does not acknowledge their sexual deviance, then someday, in some way, few expect or understand it will drive your behavior to act out inappropriately.

I believe this is true of teens being exposed regularly to Internet images that are pornographic, starting especially with adult pornography. Pornographic images have a way of searing into your brain and stimulating your hormones and chemical makeup. You may not remember your mother's birthday, but the image of the getting a $50 blowjob with a prostitute in Grand Theft Auto V is not likely to leave you soon. Think about this. There was never a need for a gaming company to introduce pornography into gaming, but they all have it. Clash of the Clans, World of Warcraft, and Grand Theft Auto. They include sex and violence to stimulate you and keep you engaged. In order to keep you coming back, it must get more violent and more sexually enticing. Most popular games include it to compete, and you can even join subgroups to talk with others who prefer to talk trash. To a twelve-year-old, that appears grown up. In addition to the fact that most children are not prepared to even acknowledge a porn addiction, let alone deal with it intelligently, the real danger is that a video game environment opens the door to thousands of predators willing and able to mold your child's thinking about sex.

They may even teach your son to question his gender choice. If that does not scare the socks off you, then I cannot imagine what would. If you think your children are addicted to pornography, then get them off the Internet while you still have some influence and go with them to get professional counseling. If you do not set the standards for what is right and moral and dignified, then I can guarantee you people you would never allow in your house will groom your child.

Children who are accessed, groomed, and recruited on the Internet *end up being exploited.*

We must do everything in our power to put the power back into parenting.

CHAPTER TEN

HOW TO REPORT AND SIGNS TO LOOK FOR

There are many situations that might indicate a young person is being groomed or recruited or is near to being exploited by a predator. Most of these signs on a standalone basis may not indicate anything at all. However, usually a person being groomed or a person already in the life will show one or more of these characteristics.

IF YOU BELIEVE THAT SOMEONE YOU KNOW IS BEING TRAFFICKED CALL 1-800-373-7888 NATIONAL HUMAN TRAFFICKING HOTLINE

1. A person all of a sudden has too much money and no way to explain it. Perhaps new clothes, nails, hairstyle, or iPad, etc.
2. New tattoos, especially of a person's name or gang brand.
3. Bruises, scratches, and cuts.
4. Signs they may be cutting themselves.
5. Unable to sleep, anxious, and agitated.

6. Goes to school and does not stay.
7. Highly emotional with outbursts and anger.
8. Attempts to run away from home or sometimes runs for a few days and returns.
9. Older boyfriend or girlfriend.
10. Teen from an alcoholic or drug-addicted home life.
11. Lying about their age or having a false ID.
12. Suddenly has a prepaid or disposable cell phone.
13. Has a stack of gift cards (this is how they pay for ads).
14. Sexually explicit profiles on Facebook or social networking sites.
15. Changes in mood: fear, anxiety, depression, anger.
16. Protects boyfriend/girlfriend even though abuse.
17. Texts using the words, "Daddy" or "Wifey." Keep the phone, don't erase, and take to the police.

UNDERSTANDING THE POWER OF SHAME-BASED BEHAVIOR IN GROOMING

The heart of the matter for all grooming and recruiting is to take control of another person's life, which provides gain for the predator. Sometimes it is financial gain, sexual domination and pleasure, and almost always the sense of being all-powerful. As you have seen from this book, there is a broad spectrum of how this plays out. Sometimes it is limited to a thirty-five-year-old getting perverted pleasure in sexting to an eleven-year-old. Even if they never meet and no physical act takes place, the Internet interaction grooms the eleven-year-old victim, who will ultimately be emotionally violated. They will most likely realize what they have done is wrong and they begin to act from a standpoint of being found and getting caught. They will most likely experience fear and shame.

Because it takes place in secret and because most children believe that what takes place on the Internet is private, often parents and professionals will realize there is something wrong, but the true situation of experiencing shame is never brought to light. In working with these children, it is important counselors and psychological professionals understand the extent to which this phenomenon is happening on the web, and take the time to stop and help the victim sort through it. Often we recognize a person's behavior has changed and we explore real life situations, but have a tendency to overlook or downplay the amount of influence and exposure a child receives when spending hours online.

The World Wide Web can be just that: a web, a trap for a naïve and unprepared young person. An innocent eleven-year-old who has been handed a smartphone, even with supervision, can and most likely will explore the possibilities. It is possible in the scenario I outlined previously where the parents entrusted their eleven year old daughter with a cell phone and then later discovered that she was sexting with a thirty-five year old man in Iowa, that the girl may have had a sense that what she was doing was wrong. I am certain that in her mind it was a harmless relationship. After all, she had not *done* anything. The mirage of social media is similar to the mirage of gaming.

Teens will tell you that they have a right to secrecy on the Internet without understanding that virtually nothing on the Internet is a secret. It is called The World Wide Web.

217

There is a double fallacy going on in these situations. Teens are being exposed to a worldwide danger without being prepared in any way, except to hear the words, "Be careful," from their parents. Without an adult standing beside them and guiding them, they are totally unprepared to deal with the myriad of snares and traps awaiting them. Our society, our parents, even our counselors are not prepared to understand the psychological impact of being accessed and groomed by a predator. Again, let's look at the case of the eleven year old above. A parent's first instinct is simply to take the phone away and punish the girl. Certainly, some of that is appropriate. What about what the girl is experiencing? Parents do not realize the impact of the grooming. This man has made sexual suggestions to this girl that she has processed and to which she has *responded.* She is obviously intrigued by the exchange. Now she has been caught. He has told her she is special in ways that no one else will understand, and she has started to believe him and build a fantasy of herself as being special to someone outside the family unit. If this scenario were being played out in person rather than on the web, we would take substantial measures to protect the child from the predator. Somehow, on the Internet we blame the girl for making herself available on the device *we* gave her, and punish her for it.

It is important at this point that the parent understand shame behavior. The girl, in her heart, knows this is wrong, but she is also starting through puberty and is mentally and emotionally experimenting with ideas of her own sexuality and value as a girl. It is important that a parent sits with the girl and shares with her that sex is not a dirty thing, but rather a valuable experience shared between two adults. Reinforce her own sense of self-worth. Okay, so she made an error in judgment, but she is not a bad person. She is not tainted. She is too important to you as a family member, and she is extremely valuable as a child of God.

In the case of the eleven year old above, there was a father in her life, and it would be helpful if he were capable of spending extra time with her and making a point of paying more attention to her. Let her know that he is her biggest fan and he believes in her. Take the time to laugh with her, tease her, and help her experience her own special value. Give her an example of how real men treat a valuable girl. Make it clear that she does not have to *do* anything to be loved. It is absolutely critical that this girl does not feel judged by her father. A father suggesting to her that she is flawed will deepen her own sense of being wounded. It will further damage her and deepen her own sense of shame. It is important that he put his arms around his little girl and tells her how important she is to him, how much he believes in her, and that he knows they will all stand together and protect each other. He will be her knight in shining armor, and she does not need to text out to strangers to experience pride in herself.

Personally, I don't believe it is wise for an eleven-year-old to have a smartphone in the first place, but since they have crossed that threshold, then I believe this could be a helpful learning experience for the whole family. It is important for them to talk about sexting (after all, at least one child knows what it is now). Explore how sexting has a negative impact on a person. Talk about how physical love can only come after you know a person well and respect them and are prepared to make a lifetime commitment to them. Basically, sexting is digital graffiti. Sexting is using meaningless terms with a person you don't know at all. It devalues the real thing. Again, reinforce with the girl that she is simply too valuable to engage in that. They might even rejoice as a family that they have all learned a great lesson and will stand together to protect each other. This way, she does not bear the entire responsibility alone and she is not isolated outside the family unit in her shame. By the way, this also allows the healing for the father, because it was his decision to purchase the phone that made it possible for his little girl to be accessed. So they both need healing.

Let me explain my reasoning for this approach. Basically, in my experience working with sex trafficking, shame-based behavior escalates into more shame-based behavior. A person feels tainted, dirty. They fear they are unlovable. They believe that what they have done is so disgusting that no one will ever understand and accept them again. It must be kept secret. They cannot tell anyone else. They cannot ask for help. Look at the case of the thousands of boys allegedly violated by errant members of the Catholic Church. Many of the male victims could not admit to their abuse for twenty years.

Shame can be a good thing. It is God's way of letting us know that we are wrong or have made a poor decision, and need to make a change in our lives. Shame in the hands of a predator, a person who is grooming a child, is called a "damaged goods trap." From that point forward, if you have fallen into this trap, all your decisions will be based on the belief that you are so flawed, so wounded, so degraded that you have no way out. Predators will build you up, lure you in, and then degrade you so you believe that you have no other alternatives. It is called "grooming."

Shame is the primary artillery of a predator. It is the "elephant in the room." It is the silent factor that makes grooming and recruitment possible. We look at the behavior, we judge, we criticize, we pretend it is not happening. It is a cancer in the soul of the victim. It will drive and control the victim's behavior, and will create an invisible emotional prison that keeps them bound even in the most violent and oppressive circumstances. Our usual response to another person's shame-based behavior is judgment, and we often respond with more shaming or rejection, driving the person deeper into the "damaged goods trap." Often in our children, we don't recognize shame-based behavior when we see it.

Let me revisit a story that I shared with you earlier in this book. A teenage daughter was a victim of sex trafficking. The girl met another girl who was new in her high school and they became friends. We now know that this was a bottom girl belonging to the Crips gang, who was placed in the high school for the sole purpose of recruiting children into prostitution. Mom told me that they began to see the girl's behavior change. At first she was defiant and starting to dress a bit different. She began to miss school, or go to school and come home early. She could not sleep. She was highly emotional. Every discussion turned into a war, but she would not talk with them about what was going on. She would just shut down or be defiant.

She began to run away from home. She ran away twice, but was home again in twenty-four hours. The family would file police reports. The third time the girl ran away, she did not come home. She was missing for over several months. The family thought she might be dead. Ultimately, she was found, rescued, and returned. She had been sold into the Rolling Crips gang in Los Angeles and was brutally exploited. Today, she is recovering, but her life will never be the same. Truthfully she is an amazing young girl and a true fighter. She is healing. She is fortunate to have a strong family with great faith to help the entire family rebuild. They are all heroes to me.

I share this story because I want to explore how shame-based behavior plays out in sex trafficking. It is the primary factor in grooming a victim, and it is the most damaging factor that keeps a victim bound. It is the silent prison that keeps them from asking for help and keeps them enslaved.

I do not know the exact details of how the bottom girl actually recruited this girl. As I have previously outlined, there are two common scenarios. Perhaps she made the concept of turning tricks and making money from casual sex appear like a lark. This often works with girls who are having sex anyway. You are doing it anyway, so why not have some fun and make some money? Everyone is doing it. In these cases, the girl goes through a psychological conviction process if she returns to a reasonably stable home with a baseline of morality. She has to start to reconcile that if anyone finds out what she is doing, she will be in trouble. She knows it is wrong, but rationalizes that it is not a big deal. She refuses to look at the degradation that is taking place when she is systematically violating her own standards.

A more common scenario is that the bottom girl took her to a party, got her drunk or high, and she engaged in sex and it was filmed. The videos or photos will be used as sextortion, with the threat of sharing them with her parents, her friends, and putting them on Facebook and circulating around the school if she does not do what they say. The girl is in a damaged goods trap. Her reactions will be similar to the case above.

I learned a lot about how this looks to a parent, as I heard this case described by the girl's mother. They were totally confused as they watched the changes in the girl's behavior. They were caring, involved, and gravely concerned parents. They had sought out counseling but could not get an appointment in time. They simply did not know what to think. They knew there was trouble, but they could not define exactly what the trouble was. As with most mothers and daughters, the mother thought maybe the girl was pregnant or maybe she was taking drugs. But neither of those scenarios appeared to fit the behavior they were observing. They had yet to be educated about shame-based behavior.

As we discuss this, let me make it clear that I am not a trained psychologist and this is not a clinical evaluation or recommendation. However, in case after case I have observed the same scenarios. I know that it is people's own sense of being violated and exploited that keeps them imprisoned. They blame themselves. Predators make the victims responsible. The victims accept this because they need to be loved. It is part of the grooming process. "*You* made me mad. *You* did not earn enough money, so I had to beat you. When your family sees these photos *you* made, *you* are disgusting and no one else will ever take you back." While all of this is extremely sad to the average person, the good news is that by understanding the process, we have the keys to unlocking the damaged goods trap.

It is all about giving up judgment and handing out *grace.*

GRACE, HOPE AND FATHERHOOD

I have been working in human trafficking for many years now. The one thing that never changes is that the only hope for victims of exploitation is grace. Originally, *Grace, Hope and Fatherhood* was written as a program to help members of the faith-based community to create programs that can prevent child sex trafficking. Though it still is, I am more and more convinced it could be an excellent personal study guide to understanding how preda-tors manipulate innocent young people, and what any concerned person can do about it.

As I stated in the last chapter, shame is at the heart of the issue. Shame is the prison that limits our ability to see our own self-worth. Our self-convic-tions, our intense guilt, our total disappointment in ourselves create a self-imposed immobility. Shame will destroy any sense of self-pride and drive us into deep despair. It often results in an individual expe-riencing a separation of personality. Most victims of sex trafficking feel they are being deeply judged and are aware that they are no longer normal mem-bers of society. Victims often say that they knew that people looked down on them. There is almost always a resignation that they are so ruined, so damaged, they simply can never go back. The longer the girl is in the life, the deeper the resignation. There is little fight for freedom left in them. At some point they might be promoted to bottom girl, and abuse and recruit new girls so they can regain a sense of power and control and be acceptable to the pimp again. It is this sense of shame and degradation that will keep girls from running even though they are being mercilessly abused.

I started with the description of how shame works in forced prostitution so you can see blatantly how it is experienced. An important goal of this book is to help you understand how shame-based behavior drives the recruitment process even in the early stages of recruitment. Even more important, I want to explore with you what we can do to keep from losing our young people, by understanding how to intervene in the shame-based grooming process.

Let's explore a typical access, grooming, and recruitment process. A young girl is on Tinder (a teen dating site). She meets a guy who says he is twenty, but he does look a little older. She is thirteen. She thinks, "How cool is that?" He is more mature and smoother than most guys her age. He tells her she is not like the other girls. She is more mature and more sophisticated. There is no way she could be in eighth grade. They text, they tweet. They exchange YouTube videos. They share some photos on Instagram. He wants to kiss her and hold her and make her feel special. Can she meet up with him? She knows better. She agrees to maybe meeting later. Well, can he at least have a photo? She thinks, a little photo won't hurt. She sends a couple of selfies with her blouse open.

He says that he loves her. They begin to sext several times a day. He wants to take care of her and give her the world. He sends her a photo of himself with an erection. She is scared and excited all at the same time. She knows it is not right. What if he just shows up at her doorstep? He is getting pushier and really wants to have sex with her for real. They begin to have phone sex and he tells her all the things he wants to do to her. Oh wow, what if her folks find out?

They will be so mad. They will scream and yell at her and maybe take her phone away. She cannot be caught. Why not? Half the children at school are "doing it." She has a right to be loved. She sends him more photos with more exposure. He says he shared the photos with a friend because she is so beautiful naked. She panics. What was she thinking? What if the photos show up on Facebook or at school or even worse, her folks see them? On and on and on.

There is nothing remotely unusual about this story. Variations play out across the Internet literally thousands of times a day. Here is the critical point.

Most parents will not recognize this girl is in shame-based behavior. How parents handle this situation is extremely critical to building trust and the self-esteem of the girl. How it is handled will define her vulnerability to being groomed in future situations.

Most fathers see their daughters as the sweet innocent child they idolized and raised. Now she is thirteen. Her hair is sprayed pink, her skirt is only twelve inches long and she has begun to swear like a sailor. She mouths off at every turn. She spends hours on the phone or computer. Deep dialogue stopped long ago. The dad loves his daughter, but he is at his wits end to know what to do. He turns to Jell-O inside (or maybe rage) and yells, "Go see your mother." Mom is as lost as dad and she says, "No way, go see your dad." The two of them stand there together, wondering where they went wrong. The first instinct for dad is to yell out, "What in the hell are you thinking?" Please don't.

In this scenario, the girl has not been physically violated (yet). However, she is still traumatized with exploitation, even if she does not realize it. Her self-esteem, her image of herself as wholesome and valuable, has been violated. Even if she is culpable, she is not mature enough to sort through the specifics.

Asking, "What the hell were you thinking?" is extremely judgmental. The girl knows what she has down is wrong. She is already panicked inside. Enduring the rejection of her father and mother will drive her directly into the boyfriend's arms. The challenge in these situations is to realize that a thirteen-year-old girl has been placed in a position where she is left to ferret out who is friend and who is exploiter. She was sucked in. She is struggling with how she could be so stupid. She fears the loss of approval of her parents, and yet it is her fantasy, she created it, and she is not prepared for the loss that will ensue when she realizes it was all a fraud. Truthfully, nothing in our society has prepared a thirteen-year-old to deal with the fallout of these inevitable situations.

As a parent, and especially as a father, I would counsel you to stop and take a deep breath. Realize the situation in total. Put aside your sense of violation and disappointment. Do not take this personally. This child did not purposely set you up to fail as a parent. This is not about you as a parent, as much as it is about understanding that this young person was placed in a vulnerable situation and introduced to predators without being equipped to protect herself. This is a teaching moment for the whole family. This scenario could be the same whether it is a son or a daughter. Shame is no respecter of persons, age or gender. Most children, when they have been sexually or emotionally violated, cannot convey the feelings related to shame. Guys especially shut down.

Regardless, parents need to take the high road and help the teen find a way out of the "damaged goods trap."

When in doubt, put your arms around your child and say, "I don't know what you are dealing with, and you may not want to talk about it. That is okay. I want you to know that I think you are hurting. When you hurt, I hurt. Whatever it is, no matter how bad it gets, I want you to know that God is going to forgive you and I am going to forgive you and whatever it is, we will be strong together. You are not alone. I believe in you with all my heart. I am proud of you." The road to recovery for your child begins with acceptance and forgiveness. Rejecting your child will only reinforce what the predator has said and drive him or her right into his arms. *It is all about grace.*

The ideal situation is that the dialogue starts long before a young person is ever exposed to smartphones, gaming, and video chat rooms. To do that means educating the adults in the family how to recognize dangers. Even more important is the concept of learning the Internet together. Parents and children looking at apps and websites and talking about the pros and cons and if they fit with your moral compass. Do they make you a better person? Do they let you be represented as a good and valuable person? Talk about the need for openness in communication, and that they should never send a photo that they would not want posted on a church bulletin board. A smart parent will learn that the Internet does not have to be a divider. It can be a catalyst for growth together.

Early on in the dialogue with teens accessing the Internet, it is important to have a conversation addressing grooming and recruitment and exploitation. Perhaps Million Kids' Facebook page could be a great tutorial. I often recommend that parents stop at the dollar store and get a little child's jigsaw puzzle. The kind with the big pieces in it. Go home and sit with your teen and take the middle piece out of it. Tell them, "This is what my life would look like without you in it. You're looking for family. Well, I am your family. You have no idea how important you are to this family. If anything ever happened to you, our lives, my life would never be the same. I hope with all my heart that nothing bad ever happens to you. If it does, I want you to know that no matter how bad it gets, no matter what happens, it is never too late to come home. It is never too late to reach out for help." I sit with parents on a regular basis that wish they had said that while their child was still with them.

For several years now, I have been talking to audiences about the "damaged goods trap." It is often the weapon pimps, bottom girls, and perpetrators will use to keep a victim in the belief they have no other choices and no one else would ever want them. It is a lie. Perhaps the most lethal lie of all. I wrote about the damaged goods trap after I met a man nearly five years ago. I had spoken at *Calvary Chapel* in Murrieta, California. I will always regret I did not get his name. He came up to speak with me after my presentation. He was probably fifty years old and a nice, quiet, humble kind of man. I will never forget. It is this man who changed my life. It is this man who I think of when I wonder what this journey is all about and I simply get too tired to keep going. It is this man who makes this work worthwhile.

He said, "My daughter is a prostitute. I know that. She has been missing for over three years. I have looked everywhere for her." He told me, "I am a truck driver. Every time I pull into a truck stop, some of the girls come up to my truck and knock on my window, trying to sell me sex. I look at every one of them. I am looking for my daughter. I do not want it to be her." I will never forget his last line. He said, "You know, I don't care where she has been and I don't care what she has done, I would give everything I own if she would just come home to me."

It is all about forgiveness and grace.

The next time you pass a streetwalker, remember she is someone's daughter and someone is probably looking for her. *She needs grace.*

CPSIA information can be obtained
at www.ICGtesting.com
Printed in the USA
LVOW12s0214131016

508557LV00001B/62/P